POWERMOM

POWERMOM

HESTER MUNDIS

CONGDON & WEED, INC. · NEW YORK

*Some of the pieces in this book appeared originally,
in other forms, in* Working Mother *magazine.*

Copyright © 1984 by Hester Mundis

Library of Congress Catalog Card Number: 84-70837

ISBN 0-86553-119-6
ISBN 0-312-92654-5 (St. Martin's Press)

Published by Congdon & Weed, Inc.
298 Fifth Avenue, New York, N.Y. 10001

Distributed by St. Martin's Press
175 Fifth Avenue, New York, N.Y. 10010

Published simultaneously in Canada by Methuen Publications
2330 Midland Avenue, Agincourt, Ontario M1S 1P7

Designed by Barbara Huntley
Cover design by Lembit Rauk
Cover illustration by Art Cumings
Cover photo by Rick Muller

All Rights Reserved
Printed in the United States of America
First Edition

WITH LOVE
for Helen Carey,
A TRUE
POWERMOM

INTRODUCTION

If you're one of those women who think that holding down a full-time job and raising a family is one of life's greatest challenges, it's time you were set straight: being a size 12 and trying to squeeze into size 8 jeans is a far greater one.

Handling two major responsibilities at the same time is no big deal. With a little effort anyone can do it. The trick is doing it with *no effort at all!* That's the difference between being a working mother and a Powermom—and being a Powermom is what this book is about.

HESTER MUNDIS
On the hypotenuse
The Bermuda Triangle, 1984

CONTENTS

PART 3: THINKING OF YOU! YOU! YOU!

Epilogue: You Are Not Alone   158

PART 1

THE HARD PARTS MADE EASY

Evaluating Your Real Feelings About Working Motherhood
Test Your Outlook on Working Motherhood

How to Sneak Out of the Office Without Losing Your Job
Substitution—Your Key to Freedom ✲ Office Exit Lines
Lunch Hour Extenders ✲ The All-Purpose Quickie
The Heavy ✲ Cautions

Eliminating Guilt
Fast 'n' Easy Ways to Get Rid of Guilt

Simplifying Household Chores
Garbage Disposal ✲ Washing Dishes ✲ Feeding Pets
Watering Plants ✲ Other Household Hints
That Mary Ellen Never Gave You

Entertaining Can Be Fun
Fast 'n' Fancy Do-Nothing Dinners ✲ Terrific Tips for
Glamorizing Meals ✲ Gourmet Meals That
You Can Prepare over the Phone

There is no such thing as a nonworking mother.
—POWERMOM PROVERB

EVALUATING YOUR REAL FEELINGS ABOUT WORKING MOTHERHOOD

Whether you're a working mother, just contemplating being a working mother, or have never dreamed of being a working mother (have never met a working mother, would rather lick stamps for a lifetime than become a working mother), the first thing to do, if you have any desire at all to be a Powermom, is to find out what your *real* outlook on working motherhood is.

For instance, as a working mother you might *think* that you never have enough time to do anything, that you can't possibly continue to pursue a career without being considered physically embarrassing by your Avon representative, mentally anorexic by your boss, and technically dead by your next birthday. Or you might *think* that nothing is more gratifying and emotionally fulfilling than doing dictation by day and diapers by night. But it doesn't matter what you *think*. Thinking isn't *feeling*. (Thinking that you have a broken leg isn't the same as *feeling* that you do.) And it's how you feel about being a working mother that counts.

TEST YOUR OUTLOOK ON WORKING MOTHERHOOD

Answer the following questions as honestly as you can. For a true evaluation, do not consult members of your family, co-workers, your horoscope, anyone else's horoscope, or the *I-Ching*.

Do you mind being awakened by ✻ ✻ ✻	ALWAYS	SOMETIMES	NEVER
✻ An alarm clock?	____	____	____
if you don't have to get up?	____	____	____
✻ Music?	____	____	____
when played by your three-year-old on a kazoo?	____	____	____
when the kazoo is stuck in your ear?	____	____	____
✻ A crying baby?	____	____	____
if it's not yours?	____	____	____
✻ A kiss?	____	____	____
if given by your husband?	____	____	____
if given by someone else's husband?	____	____	____
if given by the dog?	____	____	____
intravenously?	____	____	____
✻ Gentle tinkling sounds from the kitchen?	____	____	____
if caused by stemware hitting the floor?	____	____	____
if caused by the dog?	____	____	____

✱ A phone call?   —— —— ——
  from your baby-sitter?   —— —— ——
    saying that she's sick?   —— —— ——
    saying that she's pregnant?   —— —— ——
      by your husband?   —— —— ——
  from your grandmother?   —— —— ——
    if she's been dead for 5 years?   —— —— ——

✱ Being tickled?   —— —— ——
  by your son's rubber snake?   —— —— ——
  by your son's real snake?   —— —— ——

**When trying to get out of the house
in the morning and get the kids
off to school, do you get
upset when ✱ ✱ ✱**

	ALWAYS	SOMETIMES	NEVER
✱ Your child suddenly remembers that he needs something for a class project?	——	——	——
an unmarked $100 bill?	——	——	——
✱ You find the cat in your attaché case?	——	——	——
using it as a litter box?	——	——	——
✱ You discover that the sandwich you prepared for your child the night before was eaten the night before?	——	——	——
by your child?	——	——	——
by you?	——	——	——
by nothing human?	——	——	——
✱ Your kids start to fight among themselves?	——	——	——
with Fruit Loops?	——	——	——
with clubs?	——	——	——
to the death?	——	——	——

	ALWAYS	SOMETIMES	NEVER
✲ You can't find your makeup?	___	___	___
you find it in the fish tank?	___	___	___
you find it in your daughter's schoolbag?	___	___	___
in your son's schoolbag?	___	___	___
✲ Your child says he has a frog in his throat?	___	___	___
and it leaps out?	___	___	___
✲ Your husband has the day off?	___	___	___
and wants breakfast in bed?	___	___	___
and a back rub?	___	___	___
a divorce?	___	___	___
✲ You can't remember what day it is?	___	___	___
what month it is?	___	___	___
your name?	___	___	___

When at your job, do you become distressed when ✲✲✲

	ALWAYS	SOMETIMES	NEVER
✲ Your child phones you in the middle of a meeting?	___	___	___
to tell you about his homework?	___	___	___
for next week?	___	___	___
to tell you he's broken something?	___	___	___
a part of his body?	___	___	___
to ask you if you want to say hello to the goldfish?	___	___	___
if he's holding it in his hand?	___	___	___

✲ A neighbor informs you that she's seen your daughter in the school yard smoking?
a cigar?
a ham?

✲ You have to deal with sexual harassment?
from your word processor?

✲ You have to use your lunch hour to run annoying household errands?
for your boss?

✲ Your kids have a holiday, and you don't?
the holiday is Christmas?

✲ You realize that you've forgotten to tell the baby-sitter the name of your child's doctor?
the name of your child?

When you arrive home after work, do you become short-tempered if ✲✲✲

ALWAYS SOMETIMES NEVER

✲ You realize that you've forgotten to pick up groceries for dinner?
for the last five days?

✲ The first thing the kids say is, "What's for supper?"
when they're not your kids?

✲ The kitchen is a mess because your child has made a snack for herself?
out of Play-Doh?

	ALWAYS	SOMETIMES	NEVER
* Before you're in the house five minutes you have to take out the dog?	___	___	___
from the freezer?	___	___	___

If you answered "never" to all or most of the questions, you are either (a) lying or (b) a Vulcan. If you answered "always" to all or most of them, you are (a) on the verge of a nervous breakdown, (b) having a nervous breakdown, or (c) taking too many diet pills.

But if you answered "sometimes" to any of the above, what you really feel is that holding down a job and bringing up kids is work—which means that you're (a) normal, (b) wrong, and (c) ripe for learning the shortcuts and strategies that can make working motherhood a snap, and turn you into a Powermom!

If you leave your office because of a twenty-four-hour virus, don't get caught two hours later in the shopping mall. —POWERMOM PROVERB

HOW TO SNEAK OUT OF THE OFFICE WITHOUT LOSING YOUR JOB

An essential Powermom quality is the ability to extricate yourself at will from your job—without losing it. This is the most important skill you can acquire, though it does take practice. (True black-belt bolters can whittle an eight-hour day down to three, when necessary, and still get a Christmas bonus.) But once you get the hang of it, the more pleasure you'll get out of working *and* motherhood—especially between nine and five.

SUBSTITUTION—YOUR KEY TO FREEDOM

No matter how wonderful your job or your boss, there are definite limits to corporate understanding. Certain words and phrases, for instance, are acceptable to employers while others are not. This is where *substitution* comes in.

For example, few employers recognize the necessity of leaving the office early for a hairdresser appointment, even if you explain that there's a party that evening and your husband's ex-wife will be there. But by substituting *dentist* for hairdresser, and *excruciating pain* for party, the necessity becomes acceptably clear. Use the following as a basic guide.

OFFICE EXIT LINES

Acceptable

* I'm having a sinus attack.

* I'm coming down with the flu.

* I must reach the lab before it closes to have a blood test.

* I have a migraine.

* I have to see my doctor.

* My back is killing me.

* I'm being audited by the IRS.

* I feel faint.

* I feel nauseated.

Unacceptable

* I'm having a Big Mac attack.

* I'm going down to Macy's.

* I'd like to beat the traffic and get away early for the weekend.

* My son is an acorn in the school Arbor Day play.

* I want to see "General Hospital."

* My sofa is being delivered.

* I'm being taken out for cocktails by an old boyfriend.

* The hamster had quintuplets.

* The quintuplets are discovering sex.

✽ Female problems.*

✽ I have to pick up my mother-in-law at the airport.

✽ Female problems.*

✽ Our cat's having kittens in my lingerie drawer.

Remember that frequent or indiscriminate use of these two words can jeopardize your job and your credibility—and set the women's movement back fifteen years.

To _H. M._
Date _1/10_ Time _12:30_ A.M.☐ P.M.☒

WHILE YOU WERE OUT

M _your babysitter_

of _____

Phone _____

Area Code	Number		Extension	☒
TELEPHONED	☒	PLEASE CALL		
CALLED TO SEE YOU		WILL CALL AGAIN		
WANTS TO SEE YOU		URGENT		
	RETURNED YOUR CALL		

Message _Needs phone number for poison control center._

Operator _KB_

LUNCH HOUR EXTENDERS

Anything can happen on a lunch hour, so you're limited only by your imagination and conscience. The key is phoning in your excuse and knowing how long it will be good for. Here are some rough evaluations:

Excuse	Estimated Free Time
✻ "I broke the heel on my shoe and I'm having it repaired."	✻ Enough to try on six dresses (or four pairs of tight jeans).
✻ "I saw a cat choking on a fish bone and had to give it the Heimlich maneuver."	✻ Enough to have a relaxing facial or your winter coat remodeled.
✻ "I was hit on the head with a Frisbee and I'm going to the emergency room."	✻ Enough to watch a double feature, have an affair, or go home and make crepes.
✻ "My contact lens fell into the salad bar at the restaurant."	✻ Enough to visit an old friend, shop for new curtains, or take an EST training session.

THE ALL-PURPOSE QUICKIE

For those times when you just need an hour or two to pick up a package from a friend or talk to your child's teacher, the best way to sneak out of the office is to pretend that you're still there. What you need is an extra handbag (to play it safe, an inexpensive one) to leave on your desk. "She must be around; her purse is still here" is standard detection in most companies. You can heighten the semblance of temporary departure by leaving a full cup of coffee in view and putting

Dial-A-Joke on hold so your phone button remains lit. (NOTE: This ruse is feasible only in warm weather, unless you can figure out a way to keep an extra coat around too.)

THE HEAVY

Extreme situations require extreme solutions. If your office manager is unreasonably strict about attendance and you really want out, you can always say that your grandfather died—without mentioning that he did so six years ago. (Needless to say, if Grandpa is still alive, pick a relative who isn't.) Keep in mind that this is a one-shot. There's a limit to how many family members you can knock off without arousing suspicion.

CAUTIONS

✻ Overuse of headaches, backaches, and female problems might make you ineligible for the company health plan.

✻ Spraining any part of your body more than three times a month is excessive.

The only thing to feel guilty about is feeling guilty.
                                        —POWERMOM PROVERB

ELIMINATING GUILT

Every working mother feels guilty from time to time, and some working mothers feel guilty all the time. Powermoms know that this is not only unproductive and unwarranted, but unnecessary as well. Guilt, like mildew or unpleasant refrigerator odors, can be eliminated quite simply once you learn how.

FAST 'N' EASY WAYS TO GET RID OF GUILT

If you feel guilty about ✻ ✻ ✻

✻ leaving your infant with a baby-sitter while you go to work

✻ not being home when your child takes his first step

✻ not hearing your child say his first word

Guilt can be eliminated ✻ ✻ ✻

✻ by vividly recalling how the kid kept you up for three nights until you were ready to drop from exhaustion

✻ by checking out the prices of children's shoes

✻ as soon as the child learns the interrogative "why?"

* not having time to fix your kids a hot breakfast

* not helping your child with her homework

* letting older children come home to an empty house

* getting angry at your child when you do spend time together

* not packing a nutritional lunch for your child

* letting the laundry pile up

* not being active in the PTA

* not sharing enough experiences with your child

* being too fatigued for sex when you and your husband are finally alone together

* by fixing your kids a hot breakfast and watching them give large portions to the dog

* by spending one evening helping the kid learn the metric system (and/or the ramifications of the Dred Scott decision)

* by buying some furniture

* by recalling how long it took to remove the dog hairs from your hot rollers

* by witnessing one food fight on the school bus

* by spreading it around the house

* by not joining

* by sharing the experience of watching six "Brady Bunch" reruns

* by having sex when you're not alone or when you're not together

You can simplify any job by getting someone else to do it.

—POWERMOM PROVERB

SIMPLIFYING HOUSEHOLD CHORES

The truth about household chores is that they don't have to be chores. With a little imagination, planning, and cunning—actually no more than you need to land a job, a man, or for that matter a brook trout—you can substantially reduce the time-consuming drudgery of after-office housework. One of the best ways to accomplish this is to get your kids to do the chores.

Sound easier said than done? Well, what doesn't? If you're going to be negative, you might as well forget about being a Powermom right now.

GARBAGE DISPOSAL

Admittedly, this is a minor household task, but not one that children take to readily. Just ask a child to take out the garbage, and the typical rejoinder will be, "You expect *me* to carry *that*?" implying that you've requested a feat that under normal circumstances should be left to a forklift. (There is also, of course, the familiar "Why do *I* always have to do it?" the insidious "Gee, I'm right in the middle of my homework," and the classic "Nobody else's mother makes them do that!") This is why, in the case of taking out the trash—or with anything else that might be construed as a chore—your best approach with children is the most indirect one. In fact, the more circuitous you are, the more likely you are to succeed.

In the matter of garbage removal, gambling works best.

Kids love to bet. They'll bet on how many ants a fallen lollipop can attract in five minutes or whether or not you can wriggle your ears, cross your eyes, and rub your head at the same time; they'll bet about the staying capacity of an ice cube on a hot pavement, bubble gum on a bedpost, a playmate on his head. And all for nothing more than the joy of *winning*.

By being aware of what's often called "the Las Vegas syndrome" (or Jimmy the Greek–itis) in children, you can use it to your own advantage. For trash removal, bet your kid that he can't take it out and return to the kitchen before (a) you clean the sink, (b) you sweep the floor, (c) the clock strikes seven, or (d) you strike the kid. It becomes a sporting proposition that few youngsters can resist, and you can also use this approach to get the Christmas ornaments moved to the garage, the ashtrays emptied, letters mailed, beds made, and laundry folded. Getting dishes washed is another story.

WASHING DISHES

A more sophisticated strategy is required for getting dishes done. In the first place, it's more time-consuming than hauling out trash; in the second, it often entails dealing tactilely with used food, something that children over the age of two find very unappealing. But getting a child to rush to the sink with enthusiasm is not difficult *if* the right tactic is employed. In this instance, the right tactic is the Cracker Jack Method.

The Cracker Jack Method is nothing more than having a prize at the bottom of something (in the case of dishes, that something would be the dishwater). The offering need not be elaborate by any means. I've seen finicky five-year-olds, kids who'd rather face a firing squad than breakfast, down bales of shredded bran every morning just to reach two rubber bands and a piece of cardboard—an alleged Space Shooter with all the aerodynamic potential of wet Kleenex.

Anything that can be submerged in soap and water without harm will serve the purpose. A string of paper clips can be passed off, on different nights, as anything from an Astrokite tail to Magnet Munchies. By using your imagination, and odds and ends that have been jamming the kitchen catch-all drawer, you'll be amazed at how many dishwashing-free evenings you can enjoy.

✳ Alternative but more costly methods are buying a dishwasher or hiring a maid.

✳ An alternative but messier method is eating directly from pots with your hands.

FEEDING PETS

Kids can be easily conditioned not only to take on the responsibility of feeding pets, but to relish it, *if* they're encouraged to be creative.

You can't blame a child for balking at pushing a gelatinous cylindrical mass of unidentifiable by-products into Fido's dish. But if you show the child the potential this mass has for sculpting (some brands are more malleable than Play-Doh), it's a whole different story. The child is delighted, and in most cases so is the dog.

Our pooch (a former finicky eater who wouldn't touch his food unless we let it "breathe" for half an hour before putting it in his dish) now chows down enthusiastically on the Leaning Tower of Pisa, the Washington Monument, and, if my son is feeling *really* inspired, the U.S.S. *Enterprise* and assorted extraterrestrials.

(For further information, see "Picking the Right Pet.")

To H.M. Time 1:00 A.M.☐ P.M.☒
Date 5/1

WHILE YOU WERE OUT

M iss Wilonza
of nurse of the Bennett School

Phone

Area Code	Number		Extension
	☒	PLEASE CALL	☒
TELEPHONED		WILL CALL AGAIN	
CALLED TO SEE YOU		URGENT	
WANTS TO SEE YOU			
	RETURNED YOUR CALL		

Message Jesse had a little mishap in gym. Nothing to worry about. They've found a donor

Operator L.G.

WATERING PLANTS

Watering plants is *not* a difficult job; but for working mothers, especially after a long day at the office, the task can take on the proportions of irrigating the Negev. Defoliating the house is one way to solve the problem, but it's not easy to cast out an avocado plant you've known since its mother was guacamole. A less traumatic and more practical solution is to disguise the chore as a game.

To do this, merely replace your watering can with any squirt toy. Be it a plastic fish or an intergalactic aqua-pistol, if it sprays water and a kid is allowed to draw a bead on household flora with it, I guarantee your geraniums will never go thirsty.

OTHER HOUSEHOLD HINTS THAT MARY ELLEN NEVER GAVE YOU

Dealing with dust

✻ Allow your child to draw pictures with her fingers on dusty furniture, and then make the kid erase them. This not only takes care of the dust and keeps the child occupied, but teaches respect for household furnishings as well.

✻ While blow-drying your hair, take a few moments out from personal beautification for home beautification—give the bureaus and bookcases a blast from the dryer. You'll look as good as Scarlett O'Hara, and dust will be gone with the wind.

Coping with cobwebs

❊ Just let them accumulate and then spray-paint
them. They'll look like delicate, colorful macrame
wall hangings. Your guests will be impressed, and
you'll never have to jerry-rig an extension pole for
your feather duster again.

Fighting finger marks

❊ Buy your youngsters lightweight gloves and make
sure they wear them *indoors*. These will not only
prevent finger marks, but will help wipe away the
ones that are already there—and keep the kids'
hands clean as well.

Beating bathtub rings

❊ Forget the peroxide, bleach, and ammonia—have
the family take showers.

Painless window-washing

❊ Unless you have a view that's really spectacular,
save your sanity, spare time, and manicure—buy
shades or shutters. (If your plants need the light,
buy a grow bulb—one swish with a napkin and you
can keep it clean.)

Ironing

❊ Don't.

Eliminating red wine stains

✽ Serve white wine.

Cleaning the kitchen floor

✽ Avoid waxy buildup, housewife's knee, and the expense of a sponge mop by spilling a quart or two of milk and inviting in some friendly neighborhood cats.

Cleaning the refrigerator

✽ Go off your diet for a few days.

Dispelling unpleasant cooking odors

✽ Eat out.

Never show a guest fear—or home movies.

ENTERTAINING CAN BE FUN

It might seem difficult to put your best foot forward for company when you can barely put one foot in front of the other, but it can be done, and be fun too, if you know how to do it the easy way.

What you have to understand is this: *nowhere is it written that entertaining means providing food.* Once you accept this fact, entertaining becomes a lot simpler. For instance, even after a hard week at the office, you can relax and actually enjoy having guests by inviting them for a fast. No pots or pans to clean, no mega-shops at the supermarket, no lumpy gravies or fallen soufflés to fret about. In essence: a snap!

If a total fast doesn't appeal to you, why not a modified one? Pretzels, peanuts, and some chips and dip are always crowd pleasers. They're perfect for avoiding those dinner nightmares with orthodox vege-tarians (which inevitably occur on nights when your only unadulterated greens are pickles). Also, they eliminate the problem of leftovers, at least as long as your kids are around—which is a lot more than you can say for a lamb goulash or turnip soup, which usually wind up residing in the far reaches of the refrigerator until they look like alien life forms that phoned home and got the wrong number.

P·A·G·E
33

But if you're a confirmed traditionalist and feel that a dinner party just wouldn't be a dinner party without food, the following guide can help you become a hostess with the mostest for the least amount of work.

FAST 'N' FANCY DO-NOTHING DINNERS

The key to elegant work-free dinners is nothing more than aplomb, complete self-assurance, and the sincere desire to stoop to anything to avoid cooking. The trick is in designing a gourmet meal (which becomes known as your "specialty," thus allowing you to serve it repeatedly), a meal that under ordinary circumstances should take hours to prepare, but in your circumstances is sneakily whipped up in minutes. The menu that follows will give you the basic idea:

FRENCH ONION SOUP

VEAL CORDON BLEU

PETITS POIS

PURÉE DE POMMES DE TERRE AU GRATIN

FRAISES FLAMBÉES

FRENCH ONION SOUP
(Serves 4)

4 cans French onion soup

Heat and serve in individual dishes. (Garnish with grated Parmesan cheese.)

VEAL CORDON BLEU
(Serves 4)

4 frozen veal Parmesan TV dinners

4 slices boiled ham

Remove peas and potatoes from trays and reserve. Scrape sauce and cheese from cutlets and put aside. Place cutlets in shallow baking dish and top each with a slice of ham. Replace cheese and bake according to package directions. (Tomato sauce can be used for a quick spaghetti dinner the following evening.)

PETITS POIS
(Serves 4)

4 servings of peas from TV dinners

Heat and serve in fancy dish.

PURÉE DE POMMES DE TERRE AU GRATIN
(Serves 4)

4 servings of mashed potatoes from TV dinners

Place in baking dish and top with bits of cheese that can be inconspicuously removed from Veal Cordon Bleu.

FRAISES FLAMBÉES
(Serves 4)

strawberries for 4
4 oz. cognac

Heat cognac, ignite, and pour over berries.
    (One good shot for each guest should put the perfect capper on the meal.)

TERRIFIC TIPS FOR GLAMORIZING MEALS

Try tarragon

This is a psychologically impressive spice. Because of its odd taste (a cross between catnip and freshly mown grass), it gives any dish a unique gourmet flavor.

Splurge on sour cream

Nothing turns plain to fancy faster than sour cream. Add it to gravies, soups, salad dressings; spread it over chili or meat loaf; drop it by the ladleful over baked potatoes, freshly cooked vegetables, even an empty plate. It will add a guest-impressing note of luxury to all meals—and allow you to pass off any dish as something "*à la Russe*."

Get into creative garnishes

Don't limit yourself to the usuals (parsley, lemon and tomato wedges, orange slices, olives, etc.). For real reputation-making eye-openers, use flowers! There are few guests who'll fail to be impressed if you serve them hamburgers on a bed of roses. (Carnations go best with fish; violets with chicken.)

Top with grated cheese

No matter *what* you're serving, it will look fabulous if it comes to the table bubbling with melted cheese.

Exotic before-dinner cocktails

These are easier to prepare than exotic meals, and by the time your guests reach the table they won't care what they're eating.

Avoid "cuisine minceur" dinners

Any dish that contains more than one thousand calories *has* to be delicious.

Curry up

Whether your guests like Indian food or not, they'll never know if yours is good or bad—and will unfailingly be impressed—if you add enough curry.

Sprout elegance

Chicken burned? Quiche too runny? Never fear. The answer is sprouts. They're nature's camouflage, and will add just the right note of culinary mystery to any food you can put on a plate.

GOURMET MEALS THAT YOU CAN PREPARE OVER THE PHONE

Stuffed Pork Chops with Cinnamon Applesauce for Four

Call your mother and have her pick up 4 double-rib pork chops prepared for stuffing from the butcher. Tell her to bring the chops to your house and pick up a jar of applesauce on the way.

Have mother sauté one medium chopped onion and a cup of chopped mushrooms, then combine these with a cup of coarse bread crumbs, a tablespoon of chopped parsley, some salt and pepper, and enough sour cream to moisten the mixture.

Ask her to stuff the chops with the mixture, close the openings with toothpicks, arrange them in a baking pan to which ¼ cup of water has been added, and cover with aluminum foil.

When you get home, cook the chops for 30 minutes in a 350° oven, then uncover them and cook for 30 minutes more. Serve with applesauce sprinkled with cinnamon.

The following day, be sure to thank your mother.

Moo Goo Gai Pan for Four

This oriental specialty can be yours in minutes simply by calling your Chinese take-out restaurant. Don't forget to remove food from the little cardboard containers.

Chef Salad Supreme with Garlic Bread

Order 4 large cold-cut hero sandwiches (the kind with dressing already on them) and dismantle as soon as they're delivered.

Put the ham, cheese, salami, lettuce, tomatoes, onions, and other garnishes into a large salad bowl and add additional lettuce if necessary.

Sprinkle bread with garlic powder, slice, wrap in foil, and heat in a 350° oven for 10 to 15 minutes.

Chateaubriand for Two

Want a romantic steak dinner with candlelight and wine, asparagus hollandaise, and no fussing? Just phone for reservations at a lovely French restaurant.

The easiest way to get out of anything is usually through the door. —POWERMOM PROVERB

HOW TO GET OUT OF ALMOST EVERYTHING

It always seems like a good idea at the moment—agreeing to accompany your child's fourth-grade class to a sanitation dump, selling raffle tickets to save prospective fur coats, planning the office picnic, visiting the in-laws. But for some inexplicable reason, the instant you say "yes," you know it's a terrible idea. Psychologists are at a loss to explain this phenomenon, because "yes" doesn't run in many families. From the time most children are two, they show a definite preference for "no." Nonetheless, working mothers continually find themselves being snared in one uncompromising position after another and having to get out of them.

But not Powermoms.

Powermoms have familiarized themselves with preventive tactics and all-purpose escape routes. Once you do the same, you'll never have to worry about getting trapped again.

PREVENTIVE TACTICS
or
Things you should never say once without thinking twice

* "It's no trouble at all."

* "I *love* dogs."

* "We have plenty of room."

* "Call me anytime."

* "Is there anything I can do?"

* "I love to cook."

* "My husband is a doctor/lawyer/accountant/psychiatrist/furrier."

* "I'll try anything once."

* "Of course, bring the kids."

* "Why don't you stay for dinner?"

* "If worse comes to worst, you can use mine."

* "I eat anything."

* "Don't worry, there's more where that came from."

* "I like a man who doesn't take no for an answer."

* "How bad can it be?"

* "Over my dead body you will!"

Beware of ✳ ✳ ✳

* anything that requires only a minute of your time

* all free offers

* any solicitations that give away tote bags or T-shirts

* the following phrases:
  "Do you mind if I ask you a favor?"
  "Are you busy?"
  "Want to know what I think?"
  "Want to see the kittens?"

ALL-PURPOSE ESCAPE ROUTES

**If you want to get
out of ✳ ✳ ✳**

**Then you
should ✳ ✳ ✳**

✳ baby-sitting for friends

✳ tell funny stories about
how absentminded you are

✳ the car pool

✳ pretend to be a nervous
driver

✳ visiting in-laws

✳ get a divorce

✳ acquiring a kitten

✳ buy a dog

✳ acquiring a puppy

✳ buy a cat

✳ playing board games with
your kids

✳ let them catch you cheating

✳ baking brownies for your
kid's class

✳ buy the brownies and mash
them slightly so they'll look
homemade

✳ a dinner engagement

✳ say that you're having
domestic *problems*; fail to
mention that they're with
your vacuum cleaner

✳ a dinner engagement with
your boss

✳ change jobs

✳ a blind date

✳ casually mention that your
herpes is inactive

✳ sex

✳ see above

✳ sex with someone you love

✳ see a psychiatrist

✳ your marriage

✳ see a lawyer

✳ making breakfast

✳ sleep until noon

✳ the neighborhood

✳ move

* doing a favor

* sending Christmas cards

* licking stamps

* exercising your dog

* kissing guests good-bye

* a wet bathing suit,
quickly

* vacuuming the rug

* say that you'd love to
but . . . and follow the
phrase with anything from
"I'm expecting a package"
to "I'm expecting a baby"

* keep your arm in a sling
from Halloween on

* wear a bag on your tongue

* take it to a tennis court
and let it chase balls

* start coughing uncontrol-
lably when they get up to
leave

* grease yourself before
putting it on

* put newspapers over it and
tell visitors that it's
just been shampooed

Note: If you want to get out of a promise to a child, especially your own—forget it! There's absolutely no way to do it without destroying parental credibility, inflicting trauma, or keeping both of your legs in casts. Children *never* forget promises. It doesn't matter if they're given idly, jokingly, desperately—even as a slip of the tongue—kids cling to promises like koalas to branches, and relinquish them only with the promise of something better. Needless to say, this can lead to some pretty dangerous escalation. If, for instance, while concentrating on "Dallas" or your béchamel sauce, you unwittingly promise to take your child to see *E.T.* for the fourth time, *do it.* If you don't, you could find yourself in for two hours at the video arcade, a new Atari cartridge, and—not inconceivably—a trip to the Statue of Liberty—all the way to the head!

It's never advisable to go over your supervisor's head—unless he or she is very short.
—POWERMOM PROVERB

JOBS DON'T HAVE TO BE WORK

There's absolutely no reason to remain in a dull, unrewarding work situation, dreading Monday mornings, coming home in the evenings feeling more drained than overcooked spaghetti, hungering for weekends more than for chocolate cake or Jane Fonda's figure. Sure it's important to keep your telephone in operation, the electricity functioning, food on the table, and clothes on the kids, but by thinking like a Powermom you can do all that and have a career that you enjoy too.

FORGET QUALIFICATIONS

Just because you're a podiatrist, bookkeeper, florist, receptionist—or whatever—doesn't mean you have to *remain* one. There are thousands of jobs to choose from, and you're qualified for more of them than you think.

In fact, "qualifications" is just a figure of speech. (This is clearly illustrated by the legions of unqualified people who are now employed in such high-paying fields as the arts, politics, and auto repair.) Keeping this in mind, you should, before giving notice at your current place of business or grabbing the first better paycheck you're offered, seek a position for which you are *naturally* suited. You'll discover that by doing what comes naturally, whatever your next job, it will seem much less like work.

NATURAL SELECTION

If you're the type of mother who can easily remember which kid likes peanut butter on both pieces of bread and which likes jelly on the top half, the type who can easily whip up a dinner for six and a birthday party for sixteen, who thinks nothing of having to cook liver for the cat and toss small salads for the guinea pig, the field for you is clearly hotel management.

While it's true that many professions require specific training and skills, it's also true that many women already have that training and those skills and aren't aware of it. For instance, if you can shuttle your kids back and forth from piano lessons to soccer games, pick up your paycheck, laundry, in-laws, and the cat from the vet—all without the aid of tranquilizers— you've got what it takes to succeed in air traffic control.

DISCOVER YOUR HIDDEN POTENTIAL

Inadequacies are often qualifications in disguise. If you're totally inept with machinery, often need help to plug in the toaster, and consider being able to melt butter in the microwave a major accomplishment, there's no doubt that career opportunities await you in the repair of TVs, air conditioners, refrigerators, and other appliances.

Things that you might take for granted—handling a slumber party for five seven-year-olds in a three-room apartment, or dividing one lollipop between two kids—are actually prime requisites for employment, particularly in nuclear physics, brain surgery, and architectural design. The same holds true of being able to set a mousetrap, swat flies, and use insecticides without guilt—basic skills for anyone interested in becoming an exterminator, a mercenary, or Secretary of the Interior.

An important stepping stone to many fields is the power of persuasion, so if you're able to convince your child that Santa remembers, that the Tooth Fairy exists, and that liver on a plate is just a Big Mac in an altered state, you should certainly set your sights on becoming a real estate agent or an insurance salesperson, or on gaining the political office of your choice.

If persuasion isn't your forte, but you can still get your child to clean up his room, take out the garbage, and go to bed when you say so, you have the intrinsic talent to become either a corporate executive or a professional dog trainer.

And though men usually dominate such fields as bartending, locksmithing, and engineering, if you can untangle a Slinky and open a childproof cap without the help of your child, you can break the sex barrier and make good money as well.

JUST SAY THE MAGIC WORDS

Never forget that there are more jobs within your reach than out of it. In fact, by mastering one simple four-word phrase, you have the basic qualifications for becoming a dental hygienist, salesperson, telephone operator, librarian, secretary, radio announcer, weather person, tolltaker, butcher, baker, therapist, train conductor, jeweler, jailer, maître d', astrologer, taxi driver, stewardess, and many, many more. The phrase? *Have a nice day*, of course.

Do you have what it takes to be an actress?

If your secret desire has always been to get into acting, but your doubts about having talent have held you back, a new assessment of your abilities could be all you need.

Have you ever ✻ ✻ ✻
	YES	NO
✻ fibbed your way out of a dinner invitation?	___	___
✻ cried your way out of a speeding ticket?	___	___
✻ faked an orgasm?	___	___
✻ used imitation mayonnaise?	___	___

If you answered "yes" to two or more of these questions, you have the requisite rudiments for a career on TV, Broadway, or the big screen. Unfortunately, Tonys, Emmys, Academy Awards, and income can't be guaranteed.

Advantages	Disadvantages

ACCOUNTANT

You can balance your checkbook and budget at work and see if you're spending money foolishly.

You know that you're spending money foolishly.

ACTUARY

No one questions you about your job because they don't understand what it is that you do.

You don't understand what you do.

AIRLINE PILOT

You get to travel extensively on the job.

You never get to watch the movie.

ANTHROPOLOGIST

You get to understand the customs, culture, and social life of various civilizations and people—including your kids.

You find it difficult to make excuses for your children's behavior.

ARCHEOLOGIST

Through artifacts you learn to reconstruct human activities that happened before your time—including what your kids were up to while you were out.

You become afraid to leave the house.

BARTENDER

You get to hear all the local gossip.

Sometimes it's about you.

BUYER

You get to work in the glamorous fashion industry and buy beautiful clothes with other people's money.

You realize that you can't afford to buy the same clothes for yourself.

DIETITIAN

You become well versed in nutritional counseling and are able to give your children real reasons why they should eat their vegetables.

It's tough to sneak out to Burger King for lunch.

DOCTOR

You never have trouble reaching yourself in the middle of the night.

You always have cold hands.

FLORIST

You get to make people happy by sending them flowers every day.

They never say thank you.

HOUSEKEEPER

You earn money by performing such familiar tasks as cleaning, cooking, washing, and ironing.

You come home wishing that you earned enough money to afford yourself.

MATHEMATICIAN

You're able to intelligently help your children with their math homework.

You have to learn math.

OCEANOGRAPHER

You'll always know how to take care of the fish tank.

You'll *have* a fish tank.

Advantages	Disadvantages

PHOTOGRAPHER

You can make money attending elaborate social functions just by taking pictures.

Your friends expect you to take the pictures for free.

POLICE OFFICER

You get to master the art of criminal investigation and can tell which of your kids did what without even asking.

You find out more than you want to know.

RABBI

You have a lot of independent authority and rarely have face-to-face confrontations with the boss.

You have to work on the Jewish holidays.

RECEPTIONIST

You get to talk to a lot of interesting people.

They all want to speak to someone else.

REGISTERED NURSE

You learn to assess symptoms and aid in the treatment of a wide variety of illnesses.

You suspect that you have all of them.

TEACHER

You have summers and holidays off and get to spend that time with your own kids.

Same as advantages.

TRAVEL AGENT

You usually get to travel at substantially reduced rates.

You have fewer excuses for not bringing the kids along.

WAITRESS

You get to meet a lot of people.

All they ever talk to you about is food.

WRITER

You usually work at home.

No one believes that you're working.

To H. M.

Date 12/20 Time 1:35 A.M.□ P.M.□

WHILE YOU WERE OUT

M babysitter

of

Phone

Area Code	Number	Extension	X
	X	PLEASE CALL	
TELEPHONED		WILL CALL AGAIN	
CALLED TO SEE YOU		URGENT	
WANTS TO SEE YOU			
	RETURNED YOUR CALL		

Message Brought wrong bag of clothes to laundromat. How fond were you of fur coat?

Operator L. G.

DO'S AND DON'TS FOR NURSING POWERMOMS

Quite a few working mothers nowadays have taken to nursing their babies on the job. There's nothing wrong with this if it doesn't interfere with your duties, your child's appetite, or the company Christmas party. But if you want to be a nursing Powermom, you should acquaint yourself with some basic feeding protocol, and know how, when, and where to use it . . . to your best advantage.

If you are ✳ ✳ ✳

✳ working in an office	DO nurse your baby when asking for a raise.
✳ a lawyer	DON'T nurse your baby during a paternity trial—unless your client is the plaintiff.
✳ a teacher	DON'T nurse your baby in a class of more than five students over the age of six.
✳ a politician	DO nurse your baby (and any others that are around) during all public appearances.
✳ a professional athlete	DON'T nurse your baby while doing push-ups.
✳ a medical test volunteer or working with toxic waste	DON'T ever nurse your baby.

HOW TO MAKE YOURSELF INDISPENSABLE AT WORK

Getting fired can be detrimental to your ego as well as your bankbook, which is why Powermoms learn early to make themselves indispensable at work. The following suggestions should put you on the right track to job security.

✻ Hide the instructions for fixing important office machines.

✻ Leave out vital details when training apprentices.

✻ Memorize all the phone numbers on your boss's Rolodex, and then misplace it.

✻ Reluctantly imply that you have an incurable disease.

✻ Create problems that only you can solve.

✻ Buy the company.

HANDLING EMERGENCIES

If you're the sort of mother who fears that the worst will happen when you *are* around as well as when you're not, you can stave off panic (at least temporarily) by being prepared for a variety of emergencies. The following guide can be cut out and taped to your refrigerator, bulletin board, or any solid surface where it will be easily visible even if you're blinded by tears or rage.

GENERAL EMERGENCY GUIDE

In case of getting fired
(**a**) alert family members;
(**b**) cut all allowances immediately;
(**c**) confiscate piggy banks for duration of emergency.

In case of frog in child's pocket
Remove frog before washing clothing. (You don't want to see it after it's been through the rinse cycle!)

In case of TV breakdown
(**a**) turn on bright light;
(**b**) tell children to make shadow pictures with their hands.

In case of one missing galosh
Have child hop to school bus.

In case baby-sitter doesn't show up
(**a**) take child to lost and found office at nearest
   department store;
(**b**) leave quickly;
(**c**) check store closing hours;
(**d**) wear dark glasses when reclaiming child.
If desperate: Tie child to a parking meter and leave
youngster plenty of dimes.

To prevent child from choking
Keep hands away from child's neck.

To prevent dog from chewing child's homework
Keep homework out of dog's dish.

**To prevent child from forgetting to take lunch to
school**
Pack it in child's shoes.

**To prevent siblings from phoning you to settle
arguments**
Always judge them unfairly.

Keep these phone numbers visible

✳ Pizza parlor (that delivers)

✳ Chinese take-out restaurant (that delivers)

✳ Your analyst

✳ Dial-A-Prayer

JUST KIDDING

Kidding Around the House
Things to Keep out of the Reach of Children
Teaching Your Child Self-Discipline
Emotional Problems

Teaching Your Child Useful Skills
How Conventional Parenting Guides Have
Led Mothers Astray ✱ Keeping Powermom Child Rearing
Practical ✱ How to Teach Your Child to Ask for a Raise
How to Instruct Your Child in Tipping ✱ How to Teach Your
Child the Value of Money

Day-Care Tips for Powermoms

Improving Parent-Child Communication
Childrenese Simplified ✱ A Language That Fosters
Parental Guilt ✱ The Interchangeables ✱ The Superlatives
Numbers, Weights, and Measures ✱ The Pacifiers
Common Childrenese Phrases Translated ✱ Infantese

Going Places
Quest for Relief ✲ A Powermom's Guide to Where and Where Not to Take Children ✲ Do's and Don'ts for Taking Your Child to the Office ✲ Travel Tips

Picking the Right Pet
Minimalist Pets ✲ Living Slinkies ✲ Mickeys and Minnies Musical Pets ✲ Small and Smart ✲ A Real Playmate No Winding Required ✲ Low-Maintenance Pets

Powermometiquette
Grocery Shopping with Your Child ✲ Visiting a Co-worker's New Baby ✲ Handling Your Baby's Visitors ✲ Children's Birthday Parties ✲ Dealing with Your Child's Friends ✲ Meeting Your Child's Teacher

Coping with Clothes-Shopping for Kids
In the Beginning ✲ Know Your Times Tables ✲ The Truth About Small, Medium, and Large ✲ Import Insanity ✲ Considering the Other Alternatives ✲ The Shoemaker's Children Always Need Them—But So Do Yours ✲ Socking It to You

How to Answer Those Impossible Questions Kids Ask
Instant Impossible-Question Answer Guide

Toys That Can Harm You
What to Avoid

Teaching the Facts of Life
Powermom Facts of Life Guide

When You Should Keep Your Child Home from School

Foretelling What Your Child Will Be

Any child with two paper clips and a rubber band should be considered armed and dangerous.

—POWERMOM PROVERB

KIDDING AROUND THE HOUSE

As a working mother, you have enough to worry about without taking on the additional concern of what your children might be up to when you're not around that could cause bodily harm, social ostracism, the demise of your dinnerware, pregnancy, or an unexpected appearance on the nightly news.

Childproofing your home is the best way to eliminate this concern.

THINGS TO KEEP OUT OF THE REACH OF CHILDREN

* Sharp, glittery objects that can conceivably be forged into jewelry that you'll have to wear

* Rubber stamps and ink pads

* All riddle and pun books

* Baby brothers or sisters

* Ladders

* Old love letters

* New love letters
* Shaving cream
* Bubble bath
* Car keys (especially if child is old enough to drive)
* Plastic bags (especially if filled with chocolate)
* *Playboy* magazine (especially if you or child's teacher is the centerfold)

TEACHING YOUR CHILD SELF-DISCIPLINE

After a trying day at the office, there are few things—aside from a new litter of gerbils or the unexpected arrival of an ex-husband—that a working mother wants to face less than disciplining a child. But let's be realistic; finding your diaphragm being used as a Frisbee, the cat as a moving target for a squirt gun filled with diet cola, and the washing machine as a Jacuzzi for some guppies, you'll be hard pressed *not* to take an authoritarian stand.

Spanking is not necessarily the answer

Spanking is usually the first thing that comes to mind, though personally I am not in favor of it (except, perhaps, between consenting adults for recreational purposes, but that's another story). This is not to say that Powermoms are confirmed spare-the-rod-and-spoil-the-child types; but spanking is a sort of family-style capital punishment and should only be used as a last resort and for a very good reason.

Some very good reasons ✻ ✻ ✻

✻ Arson (especially if it's your home)

✻ Force-feeding the cat . . . to the dog

✻ Lying (but only if on new furniture with dirty sneakers)

✻ Flashing at Little League games

✻ Playing dentist with baby's new teeth

✻ Performing an indecent act with any household appliance

✻ Short-circuiting grandfather's pacemaker

✻ Hijacking a school bus

✻ Slouching and/or talking with a mouth full of food

Spanking a child because she is crying (which often occurs soon after a working mother arrives home, and regularly at supermarket checkout counters) is ridiculous. It makes as much sense as giving the Heimlich maneuver to a hunger striker. Nonetheless, there are mothers who not only spank their children for crying, but spank them again because they don't *stop* crying. Naturally if the kid is being hit, she is going to cry.

What's really upsetting about spanking is hearing a mother say, "This hurts me more than it hurts you." Now, come on. It does not! If it did, and the mother really wanted to dole out punishment, she'd have the kid spank her. Not that guilt isn't an effective disciplinary weapon, but it should be used only when such conventional methods as threats, TV curfews, and the enforced wearing of wool underwear don't work.

Using guilt as a disciplinary method

When child doesn't remember to pick up toys

YOU SAY: "Oh, no. Leave them right were they are. If anyone trips over them and breaks a leg, it'll probably only be just me—your mother. . . ."

When child balks at taking out the garbage or bringing in the groceries

YOU SAY: "Forget it. Forget I even asked you. It's (they're) not that heavy, and my back isn't hurting as much as it was yesterday, and I probably won't even need that brace if I'm careful, so don't worry about it—I'm only your mother. . . ."

When child doesn't want to help with the dishes

YOU SAY: "Sure, go out and play with your friends. I've worked all day, rushed home to make you dinner, feel as if I'm ready to drop from exhaustion—and probably will—but you shouldn't let that bother you. I'm only your mother."

So what's the answer? Teach your child self-discipline! Unfortunately, children can't be supervised every moment, and certainly not by busy moms, so it's important that a child be taught early on how to make proper decisions about his own behavior based on past experience and well-set family guidelines.

To do this, the child must be given boundaries and know what's okay to do and what's not, as well as the consequences for the latter.

Sample boundaries

It's okay ✻✻✻

✻ to color pictures in a coloring book

✻ to play gently with the cat

✻ to take cookies and milk when returning home from school

✻ to ride a bicycle slowly

✻ to excuse yourself politely from a room

✻ to play board games with your friends

✻ to use your allowance to buy what you want

✻ to hang things up in your room

But not okay ✻✻✻

✻ to do it with mommy's lipstick

✻ in the bath

✻ to take them from your friends

✻ over your brother

✻ during a math test

✻ to use real boards

✻ if what you want is controlled substances

✻ if any of those things are alive

Sample consequences

✻ Spanking   ✻ No dessert   ✻ Confiscation of video games
✻ Grounding   ✻ No TV
✻ No allowance ✻ Being sent to room   ✻ The rack
✻ No junk food

Once a child learns what's right and what's wrong and knows which punishment fits what crime, he will be able to discipline himself. (Any youngster capable of sending a perfume bottle to the floor can send himself to his room.)

Having self-disciplined children not only frees you from a hefty emotional burden but affords you the comforting knowledge that, no matter what havoc they wreak while you're at work, when you arrive home they'll already have spanked themselves, turned off the TV, and resigned themselves to a week without allowance and/or dinner without dessert.

EMOTIONAL PROBLEMS

Discipline problems in children often stem from emotional problems, which is why it's important to recognize the warning signals of emotional unrest.

First-alert warning signals of emotional problems in your child

The child ✳ ✳ ✳

✳ orders a salad at McDonald's

✳ prefers "The MacNeil/Lehrer Report" to "The Dukes of Hazzard"

✳ eats a peanut butter sandwich with a knife and fork

✳ leaves in the middle of *E.T.*

✳ is afraid to take the Pepsi challenge

✳ sets traps for the Easter Bunny

✳ wants to grow up to be a piña colada

✳ plays doctor with a real scalpel

✳ sleeps late on Christmas morning

✳ forgets his own birthday

✳ worries about retirement

* never looks for the prize in cereal or Cracker Jack boxes

* goes to bed without being told

* never asks "why?"

* wants to experience life after death

A mind is a terrible thing to waste—but then so is leftover turkey.   —POWERMOM PROVERB

TEACHING YOUR CHILD USEFUL SKILLS

The most important aspect of child rearing is preparing kids for adulthood. They need very little help with childhood. (Most youngsters learn to crawl backward, throw things, remove childproof caps, and write their names in various substances on the walls all by themselves.) In other words, whether or not you spend five selfless months with boxes of flash cards and colorful blocks teaching your child the alphabet, the kid is going to have A to Z down pat when graduating from high school, if not sooner. This also holds true for tying shoelaces, telling time, brushing teeth, and staying dry through the night, clearly indicating that working mothers have been wasting a good part of their quality time—and their children's formative years—on nonessential instruction.

HOW CONVENTIONAL PARENTING GUIDES HAVE LED MOTHERS ASTRAY

One of the first games a mother is supposed to play with her baby is "Where is mommy's nose?" This awareness game has been universally accepted as an important learning experience for children. The child points to mommy's nose, her eyes, her mouth, her chin, and forevermore knows where they are located. Indeed a learning experience, but certainly one of questionable long-range importance. Mommy's nose, one hopes, will always be in the same place, and I can't imagine any adult who'll often be called upon to locate it.

When you consider the time and energy expended by both mother and child on this impractical pastime, the need for revision is evident—which is where Powermom Child Rearing comes in. Instead of asking the child, "Where is mommy's nose?" the question should be "Where is mommy's car key?" or "Where is mommy's other earring?" or "Where is mommy's briefcase?" or any number of other sensible queries that would not only have relevance but also train the child to be of invaluable assistance to his mate (as well as his mother) in the years to come.

KEEPING POWERMOM CHILD REARING PRACTICAL

✳ Spend less time teaching your kids the parts of their bodies and more time teaching them the parts of cars. When they grow up and have a pain, they can always point to where it hurts; when their car has a problem, they'll have to *pay* someone to locate it. Knowing a carburetor from a camshaft can be far more useful to the average adult than being able to distinguish between a toe and an elbow (any adult who can't tell a toe from an elbow shouldn't be driving a car anyway), and it's common knowledge that it's easier to find a good doctor than a good mechanic.

✷ Focus instruction on things that can help a child as a grown-up. For instance, how to ask for a raise. Once your youngster enters the business world, that knowledge far outranks the ability to tie shoelaces. (Very few successful businesspeople wear shoes with laces these days anyway.)

How to teach your child to ask for a raise

All you need do is explain one basic rule: there are right times and wrong times to ask for anything. Use illustrations such as "If mommy is in the bath, on the phone, kicking cabinet doors, muttering, screaming, hurling breakable objects at the floor or any member of the family, it's a *wrong* time; if mommy is singing, dancing with the floor mop, or offering cookies for no reason at all, it's a *right* time." When your child matures, she should be able to make the transition from Parent to Boss easily, and in the long run go much further than other kids who spend half their preschool years learning which little piggy went to market.

✷ Remember that it's as important for your child to learn about savoir faire as it is to learn about bus fare. Not knowing the cost of public transportation can result, at worst, in missing a ride; saying or doing the inappropriate thing at a dinner party can cause deep feelings of social inadequacy and result in uncomfortable episodes of insomnia, usually accompanied by the sinking sensation that one might be a nerd.

✷ As soon as children are old enough to count, teach them who, when, and how much to tip.

How to instruct your child in tipping

Hold out your palm every time you serve dinner, drive the kid to a friend's house, or clean up the mess in the playroom. (Using fake money is best, since children are innately possessive about their own legal tender.) If the tip you receive is inadequate, scowl; if it's sufficient, smile politely; if it's generous, give the child a hug and remember to call her by name at every encounter during the next two weeks.

To _H. M._
Date _8/8_ Time _10:10_ A.M.☐ P.M.☒

WHILE YOU WERE OUT

M _your son Jesse_

of _____

Phone _____

	Area Code	Number	Extension ☒
TELEPHONED		☒	PLEASE CALL
CALLED TO SEE YOU			WILL CALL AGAIN
WANTS TO SEE YOU			URGENT
	RETURNED YOUR CALL		

Message _Wants to know how to remove nail polish from teeth._

Operator _L.G._

✻ Avoid standard bedtime stories. It's okay to ply kids with tales of how the early bird catches the worm, if the children are being groomed to be ornithologists or fishermen; but devising your own stories about how the clever commuter catches the train, how the caller who phones after six saves money, or how the smart shopper clips coupons and remembers to take them when going to the supermarket will provide enlightenment of a more useful variety.

✻ Put more verisimilitude into math training. Rephrase such problems as "How many pieces of pie were eaten if Sally ate two and Bobby ate two?" to emphasize the addition that really counts—calories!

How to teach your child the value of money

Having a kid drop coins into a piggy bank is a poor form of demonstrating that a penny saved is a penny earned, since banks of this type don't pay any interest (and rarely give away toasters to new depositors). Even as a toy, these banks have drawbacks. The hole in the bottom, where money can be reclaimed by the child at will, fosters a dangerously false sense of security. More effective would be a play parking meter or laundromat or broken soda machine—something with no hole at the bottom, that could impress upon the child that even if the money is well spent, it's still gone forever.

✻ Select toys that can teach your child something useful. Putting together a three-piece wooden giraffe—no matter how educational the manufacturer claims it to be—is *not* going to prepare your child for dealing with the IRS (or even a change-of-address notice, for that matter). In fact, if educational toys were really *educational*, they'd teach kids things like how to balance a checkbook, fix a clogged drain, or take stains out of silk blouses.

✳ Don't waste time showing your kids how to make peanut brittle; teach them how to make a good cup of coffee instead. There's nothing wrong with peanut brittle, but I haven't had a friend stop by for it in over twenty years.

When good day care is hard to find, a night job helps.
—POWERMOM PROVERB

DAY-CARE TIPS FOR POWERMOMS

✻ It's best *not* to leave your child in any home that has more than six locks on the door, an animal kept on a chain, or a fish tank containing dead guppies or live piranhas.

✻ It's bad form to ask for a receipt when dropping your child off at a day-care center.

✻ It's unwise to employ a baby-sitter who takes drugs—especially if she takes them from your medicine cabinet.

✻ Be wary of hiring anyone you've seen more than once wearing Band-Aids or a cast.

✻ Be wary of retaining anyone you've seen more than once wearing your jewelry.

✻ It's counterproductive to employ a day-care person whom your child has to help cross the street or feed.

✻ Never fire the baby-sitter—until you get home.

Before attempting to communicate with a kid,
try getting through to your Water Pik.

—POWERMOM PROVERB

IMPROVING PARENT-CHILD COMMUNICATION

One thing more frustrating than being in a foreign country and finding yourself unable to speak the language is being in your own home and finding yourself in the same predicament—encountering Childrenese, a language you can be fluent in around age three, use extensively up to about sixteen, and then totally forget when you become a parent.

To be a Powermom it's important to learn Childrenese, but it's not easy. This doesn't mean that it's difficult, just that translations are up for grabs. (The communication gap between parents and kids makes the Grand Canyon look like a skid mark.) All you have to keep in mind is that what kids say often has nothing to do with what they mean, and what they mean often has nothing to do with what they say. Once you get that down, you've got it made.

CHILDRENESE SIMPLIFIED

To begin, let's take a statement like "I'm not hungry." Under ordinary circumstances the meaning is perfectly clear; the speaker is without appetite. But if the speaker happens to be speaking Childrenese, ordinary circumstances (to say nothing of logic, compassion, and absence of malice) don't apply. When a kid says, "I'm not hungry," it could mean "I know we're having liver for dinner" or "Alex and I haven't finished our Monopoly game yet" or "You wouldn't let me go out to play with my friends, so I'll show you." The time to take the phrase literally is when the kid says it in a pizza parlor or a McDonald's, or when face to face with a batch of freshly baked chocolate chip cookies.

Another straightforward expression that becomes idiomatic in Childrenese is "I'm not tired." As simple and declarative as it appears, it has nothing at all to do with the child's actual physical state. A kid might have glazed eyes, look as if he's spent the day running up and down the World Trade Center playing Beat-the-Elevator, and still say he's not tired if the TV movie he's watching continues past his bedtime. And he'll hold to it, no matter what the hour or what he's doing, as long as a younger sibling is still awake. A ten-year-old boy would sooner slash his bicycle tires than go to sleep before his baby sister.

Declarations denying well-being, like those denying fatigue, need no basis in physiological reality. Barring a fever, a pallor akin to skim milk, spots, blotches, tonsils the size of golf balls, or demonstrable evidence of intestinal unrest, it's safe to translate "I don't feel well"—along with its variations, "My throat hurts," "My stomach aches," and "I think my foot's broken"—as "I didn't study for the history test," "You're not getting me to Aunt Rita's," or "That's too many dishes for anyone to wash."

A LANGUAGE THAT FOSTERS PARENTAL GUILT

A familiar Childrenese expression, vocalized ritually on Saturdays, Sundays, holidays, and sick days—and one that should never be taken literally—is "There's nothing to do." This is uttered simply to instill parental guilt. (See "Eliminating Guilt.") It implies that you've bought the wrong toys; taught self-reliance improperly; that you've failed somehow. What it *really* means is that there's nothing on TV the kid likes, her best friend is sick and can't come visit, or you've squelched her plan to make confetti in the food processor.

Instilling guilt or feelings of inadequacy in parents is integral to Childrenese, as natural as rolling *r*'s in Spanish. A kid can make you feel inadequate anytime, anyplace. My niece Dawn makes her mother feel inadequate in clothing stores (and her mother is a buyer for Lord & Taylor!). She does it with three little words: "It doesn't fit." There would be nothing wrong with this statement if, in fact, the garment the kid was trying on didn't fit; but it usually does, and her mother can see that as well as the harried salesperson waiting on them can. But Dawn prefers to say, "It doesn't fit," even though she means "I don't like it," "It itches," or "They're not designer jeans." She's eight and more comfortable speaking in her native tongue.

"Everybody else's mother lets them" is another uppercut to your self-confidence. It's used as the standard rejoinder to any parental "no." But, Power-moms, do not be intimidated! Stick to your negative guns! There is strong statistical evidence attesting to the fact that everybody else's mother does not let her child launch model airplanes from the roof . . . raise tadpoles in the bathtub . . . buy a boa constrictor . . .

take John Lennon's birthday off from school . . . eat pizza for breakfast, or sleep with the hamster.

"Nobody else's mother . . ." is another popular phrase, intended to make you feel singularly cruel, as if you should run out and trade your crock pot in for a caldron. I might have done so long ago had I not found it difficult to believe that *nobody* else's mother ever asked her kid to rake leaves, make the bed, or take more than one bath a week.

THE INTERCHANGEABLES

In Childrenese, interchangeable words and phrases are ethical, grammatical, and acceptable. Two favorite wintertime expressions, "It's not cold out" and "It's cold out"—which have nothing to do with Fahrenheit or centigrade realities—are sometimes used within minutes of each other, depending upon what's happening outside, and who's doing it. When a child says, "It's not cold out," it means that he doesn't want to put on a sweater, hat, snowsuit, boots, or other obvious concession to parental concern. If he says, "It's cold out," there are no playmates around or you've asked the kid to walk the dog.

THE SUPERLATIVES

Superlatives are staples of this esoteric language, and statements incorporating them are usually followed by the phrase "in the world." The trick to being a Powermom is not to be intimidated or overwhelmed by them. Over the years, my children have introduced me to the smartest kid in the world, the best speller in the world, the funniest girl in the world, the toughest boy in the world, the fastest talker in the world, and numerous remarkable others, all of whom have been omitted from *The Guinness Book of World Records* by some curious oversight.

NUMBERS, WEIGHTS, AND MEASURES

Numbers are fairly standardized in the language of the young: there are either a hundred or a million of any quantity of things that cannot be counted at a glance. The smaller or more objectionable the object, the larger the estimate. Thirty green beans on a kid's plate will be called one hundred. Twenty ants on a fallen candy bar will be counted as a million. (To find the actual number of pebbles in your daughter's shoe, take the number she gives you and divide by two. To learn how many cookies your son has eaten, multiply whatever he tells you by five. It's confusing at first, but after a while you get the hang of it.)

The concept of weight is conveniently simplified. If something takes effort to lift and the child doesn't want to carry it, it "weighs a hundred pounds." If, on the other hand, the object to be lifted is a present for the kid—be it a dollhouse or a canoe—it will be deemed "light as a feather." Brown paper bags holding garbage or groceries always weigh one hundred pounds. Anything gift wrapped is light as a feather.

THE PACIFIERS

Probably the most difficult parts of speech to master in Childrenese are the pacifiers. These are confusing and used only to subordinate parental requests.

Pacifiers incorporate such words as "later" (which means "never"), "soon" (which means "later"), "never" (which could mean "tomorrow"), and "just this once" (which sets a precedent you'll be unable to break). What's interesting to note, though, is that while pacifiers have their origins in Childrenese, they've also come to be accepted in adult communication through common usage by parents, repair persons, Hollywood agents, and politicians.

Keeping this simple guide to Childrenese in mind, you should find that when all that can be unsaid is done, you'll at least have no trouble understanding it.

Common Childrenese phrases translated

What they say ✳✳✳	What they mean ✳✳✳
✳ "Jason is the most selfish kid I know."	✳ "Jason wouldn't give me his lunch."
✳ "Would you like some help with the dishes?"	✳ "I failed my social studies test."
✳ "You're the best mom in the whole world."	✳ "Thanks for the ten bucks."
✳ "What makes you think I'd do something like that?"	✳ "How'd you know I did something like that?"
✳ "It was just a little accident."	✳ "The stemware's gone."
✳ "I think there's something wrong with the sink."	✳ "My crayons fell down the drain."
✳ "It's nothing."	✳ "It's something."

Infantese

It's a known fact that lawnmowers make more intelligible sounds than many one-year-olds, yet ironically most mothers are skilled translators of Infantese, a language that any reasoned linguist would admit is far more difficult to master than basic Turkish or any of the Chuckchean tongues of northeastern Asia. For instance, when a nine-month-old crawls up to his mother and says, "Wa googoo," it's quite impressive to hear the mother offhandedly explain that her child wants a cookie. It's even more impressive when you're in a room with five mothers and five infants, all using different words to request the same cookie, and each mother translates with equal aplomb. The rough estimate for nine-month-olds is that there are somewhere between twelve and one thousand words for cookie. And that's in English!

Conversely, the infant word "baba" has countless interpretations. In my own circle of friends, "baba" has been translated for me as "See the baby," "That is my brother," "I want my bottle," "I don't want my bottle," "Where is my bottle?" "Hi, Uncle Bernie," "book," "ball," "Big Bird," "May I have a bite of your bologna sandwich?" and "Here comes the bus."

Never travel with a child under any circumstances other than an assumed name.

—POWERMOM PROVERB

GOING PLACES

Traveling anywhere with a child is risky; traveling anywhere you plan to return to is even riskier. For this reason, it's essential to familiarize yourself with the possible pitfalls that await you on any outing with your youngster.

QUEST FOR RELIEF

No matter how diligent you are in making sure children have enough time to accomplish everything before leaving home, it's a rare kid who completes a shopping trip—or any other kind—without a tug of your sleeve and a whisper. (For reasons that continue to drive mothers to Spock and spur doctors and psychiatrists to wild hypotheses, children have a compulsion for checking out bathrooms that is rivaled only by their curiosity about sex, death, and Christmas presents.) The standard parental rejoinder of "Why didn't you go before we left?" is easily countered with "I didn't have to" or the real stopper, "I did." In either case, it's up to you to find a bathroom, which all too often turns into an odyssey worthy of Homer.

Rest rooms, loos, johns, w.c.'s, lavatories, the ladies' room, toilets, facilities, whatever you want to call them—their names are legion, but their number is small. In fact, rarely have there been so few for so many. And like policemen and taxis, they're never around when you need them.

To ferret out a rest room for yourself is an inconvenience, but when it's for your child it can be a nightmare, and a recurring one at that. If you happen to be on the brink of toilet training your toddler when this occurs—a time when every success brings you closer to diaper-free living, and a failure on your part could traumatize the kid for life—you enter a whole new world of anxiety. You become as desperate as a boxing manager whose fighter has only one more round to go. "Hang on, you can wait just a little longer. Mommy knows you can." "We'll get there soon." "Just a few more minutes and we'll find one."

Anxiety levels vary according to circumstances. Boys, for instance, pose a particular problem for mothers where rest rooms are concerned. Around the age of six they're no longer comfortable being taken into the ladies' room, and you're not quite ready to let them fend for themselves in an area to which you're denied access. An area that has in fiction and fact been presented as a veritable snake pit of perversity. (The first time my son used a men's room, I stood outside and tried to convince myself that it was irrational to believe that every man who followed him in was a child molester; but rationality has never pacified me. By the time my kid emerged, *I* needed a rest room.)

Taking a child with you into most available public facilities is no picnic either. Trying to watch your purse and balance a three-year-old on one of those seats might be a snap for contortionists, but it's a muscle wrencher for ordinary moms. It's especially challenging for those mothers who have had drilled into them, from earliest memory, a dire warning, a warning passed on from mother to child, a warning as hard and fast as not taking candy from strangers: DON'T SIT DOWN! (To this day I am not sure what diseases lurk in public toilets; but unless I come across a weirdly lit sanitized seat, the kind that springs back if you don't move quickly, I still heed my mother's dictum—and remember to flush with my foot as well.) Nevertheless, the real problem is not what happens when you get there, but getting there itself.

An informal poll of relatives, friends, and absolute strangers has confirmed what everyone who has ever left home with a child in tow has always suspected—that there are good and bad places to get caught.

The good, the bad, and the expensive

The worst place to get caught, with or without a child, is a drugstore. Modern outlets for products as removed from medicine as books, Silly Putty, and rain boots, drugstores convey the feeling that they can fill all your family needs—except, of course, *that* particular one. Frequently, drugstore employees will tell you they don't have a bathroom. This is an outright lie. Ask them where they wash their hands, and they'll come around quick enough. But then they'll explain that you can't use it because it's in the back where the drugs are. If your child is under eight, your chances of getting them to relent are better than if the kid is nine or over. (The odds of a five-year-old ripping off a gross of Valium are definitely in the store's favor.)

On the brighter side, there are department stores. Unfortunately, their brighter side dims on Thursday nights and during the holiday season. Those times you and your youngster can find yourselves waiting in line for a toilet as long as you would for a hit movie. (If you need a tampon, forget it. Whoever fills those machines is obviously convinced that the menstrual cycle comes around about as often as Halley's comet.) But the rest rooms are there, and you can use them and send your kids into them with relative confidence and without having to resort to a costly ruse. The latter, regrettably, is what many of us have been driven to in moments of crisis. It's what you have to do when your four-year-old begins walking with her legs crossed, and you're between a parking lot and a Chinese restaurant whose facilities are restricted to paying customers. It's hustling the kid into the restaurant, walking briskly to the bathroom, and tossing an order for a small won ton soup over your shoulder as you go. Of course, you're stuck with the soup; but that's better than what you'd deal with otherwise. My friend Helen, an accomplished Power-mom, figures that she's bought about thirty undrunk cups of coffee, forty-six unsipped sodas, and two gallons of untouched won ton soup during the past fifteen years of rest-room questing with her four kids.

They might have outlawed the pay toilet, but not for mothers who get caught with four-year-olds between a parking lot and a Chinese restaurant.

Butcher shops, bakeries, and dry cleaners, though not as bad as drugstores, are still strategically unfeasible places to be when you're in need. Even though you know better, these establishments always give the appearance of not having bathrooms.

The pits stops

Supermarkets hide their bathrooms (and when you find them you realize why). These are for store personnel only, but a friendly checkout clerk will usually direct you to one. The problem is, when you finally navigate past the towering cartons of tomato juice, creamed corn, and paper towels and arrive with your child at your destination, you will most likely have second thoughts about shopping at that market again. One would think that an establishment with a whole department dedicated to cleansers and household necessities could mop the bathroom and equip it with toilet paper. It's a small consolation to see that the sign on the door insists that all employees wash their hands thoroughly before leaving.

Unsanitary-looking facilities are by no means restricted to supermarkets. Gas stations may keep their pumps spiffy, but it is a rare pit stop that doesn't trigger a longing for the open road.

Be prepared

So rare are public conveniences that some Powermoms keep mental notes on locations. I've met one fantastically organized working mother of three who has a map of the rest rooms at her local mall, as well as a guide for the major shopping areas in five cities. Only a brave (or foolish) mother sets out with her child after a Saturday lunch with three glasses of juice to alien territory; only an even braver (or more foolish) mother-to-be.

Unfortunately, the only places you can be assured of finding really convenient and sanitary facilities are on airplanes, luxury liners, and at expensive restaurants—but if you're really a Powermom, you know that those are the places you go when you *don't* want your kids along.

A POWERMOM'S GUIDE TO WHERE AND WHERE NOT TO TAKE CHILDREN

Places to take children

* school
* camp
* their friend's house

* the dentist
* the doctor
* the baby-sitter

* Mr. Rogers' Neighborhood
* Grandma's house

Places not to take children

* on your honeymoon
* pet shops
* your boss's house

* on a job interview
* your Lamaze class
* an archeological dig

* a desert island
* Fantasy Island
* Three Mile Island

DO'S AND DON'TS FOR TAKING YOUR CHILD TO THE OFFICE

Kids always want to see where their mom works, and mothers who don't know better always want to show off their kids. It's an instinct; but lemmings have similar instincts, and if you can fight it—do! The way children behave at home is no guarantee of how they will behave at your office. I have seen four-year-olds do things to typewriters that you wouldn't want done to war criminals. The boss's kids can get away with it, but try explaining to management that your child thought the switchboard was a new kind of video game—and don't hold your breath for a Christmas bonus.

* DO try to have the child visit when your boss is out of town.

* DON'T have the child visit if your boss is out of tranquilizers.

* DO instruct the child to call your boss by his or her formal name.

* DON'T let the child call your employer by any of the names the kid might have heard you use around the house.

* DO bring along a few toys for the child to play with.

* DON'T bring along anything musical, squeakable, or live.

* DO explain your job simply.

* DON'T explain it so simply that the child can do it.

Travel tips

Being in any confined space with a child is a potentially hazardous situation. Whenever possible, avoid libraries, religious institutions, buses, elevators, prisons, and tombs. (On the street, when your kids do something embarrassing, you can pretend you don't know them—but in close quarters, when they're holding your hand, it's a tough thing to pull off.)

* Use stairs whenever possible (you can always lag a step or two behind the kid).

* Practice the phrase "They're not mine!"

If using public transportation, take the fastest. (A child on a long journey with a virtually captive audience is capable of more social indiscretions than a flasher with a new raincoat.)

* Never travel with a child who brings along anything that can conceivably melt, leak, bite, or detonate on contact.

It's wise to avoid any pet that might require glasses, orthodontia, analysis, or its own TV.
—POWERMOM PROVERB

PICKING THE RIGHT PET

Almost every kid wants a pet sooner or later. This is a fairly standard phase in children's growth. But what mothers often don't realize is that this is one area of development where *later* is better. Few aspects of working motherhood are as trying as premature pet acquisition.

But whether it's sooner or later, admitting a member of the animal kingdom into your household will always pose some problems. The only way to avoid the problems is by avoiding pets entirely. Unfortunately, this can only be done by never encouraging a child to pet the "nice kitty" or "doggie," by foregoing zoo outings, and by eliminating all bedtime stories involving animals in comic, romantic, or heroic situations. Since this is not just unnatural and cruel but impossible as well, your best bet is to make a wise choice.

MINIMALIST PETS

Because nature's emporium offers such a vast selection, the first thing a pet-choosing Powermom should do is narrow down the possibilities. The simplest way to do this is to choose the phylum most suited to you, your home, and your child. Sponges (Porifera) tend to be overlooked in this initial winnowing, which is a big mistake. No pets could be easier for youngsters to take care of.

A sponge (and there are hundreds of varieties) is an aquatic animal that requires minimal care, company, and food. It's perfectly suited for a home where there are young children, who often squeeze, drop, or step on a pet unwittingly. A sponge requires no immunization shots, doesn't shed, and will never chew up the living-room couch when you go out. It makes a wonderful bath playmate, and because it's not demonstrably active, your child will never even know when it's dead. (This eliminates the whole pet-funeral business, which always runs into snags when you can't find an empty shoe box.)

Mollusks, such as snails, are also easy-to-keep companions for kids, especially less active ones. When bought in pairs, snails can be quite entertaining. By drawing a "start" and "finish" line on the outside of their aquarium or terrarium (depending on the type of snail), your child can while away many, *many* hours watching these cute slowpokes race. (Giving them names such as "Speedy," "The Whiz," or "Lightning" adds to the fun.) Land snails can be picked up and played with, but because of their size—about that of a large gumdrop—they're not recommended for kids under three years of age.

LIVING SLINKIES

Another ideal pet for children who aren't old enough for real responsibility (to say nothing of working mothers, who have too much responsibility already) is the earthworm. Youngsters can be delighted easily by the in-hand wriggles of this svelte natural contortionist. It makes a fine apartment pet, requiring little more than a can of moist dirt for lodging. Inexpensive and hardy, it's one of the most portable members of the animal kingdom. Because the earthworm adapts well to climatic changes, it's one of the few pets you can take on both long family trips and short bus rides. Best of all, in the event your child tires of it, the earthworm can be returned to its natural environment with no trauma at all.

Snakes, though longer and more elegant than their earthworm cousins, do not make nearly such care-free pets. They're sensitive, moody, more like writers than reptiles (even nonvenomous ones will nip when piqued), and are difficult to leave with a neighbor when you have to go out of town. Aside from teaching kids bad habits, such as sticking out their tongues, most snakes require a live diet—frogs or mice for the large ones—which can present moral questions at feeding time that most mothers are unprepared to answer. One mother I know allowed her son to buy a boa constrictor only on the condition that he alone would deal with its feeding. What happened on the very first day, though, was that the kid grew so attached to the mouse he'd brought home for the boa that he wound up returning the snake and keeping its lunch as a pet.

MICKEYS AND MINNIES

In households that have no cats or snakes, mice do make excellent pets—but they have their drawbacks. As tameable as they are, mice have to be watched every moment when being played with, or they'll take off on their own and turn the area behind your kitchen cabinets into a comfy condominium. They resemble hamsters physically, and, like hamsters, mice instinctively tend to hide away a portion of their food—a habit that tends to draw flies, which do *not* make good pets. Then again, flies might come in handy if your child also has a pet lizard, spider, or frog—though personally, I am against keeping a food chain in one's own private residence.

To _H. M._ Time _4:40_ A.M.☐ P.M.☐
Date _7/3_

WHILE YOU WERE OUT

M _The Veterinarian's_
of _Office_
Phone _____
Area Code — Number — Extension

TELEPHONED		PLEASE CALL	X
CALLED TO SEE YOU		WILL CALL AGAIN	
WANTS TO SEE YOU		URGENT	
		RETURNED YOUR CALL	X

Message _Your cat Oscar is fine. You might consider a name change when the kittens arrive._

Operator _L. G._

MUSICAL PETS

Musical pets are always fun, and kids respond
particularly well to them. But since most songbirds
are expensive, intrinsically frail, and demanding of
care, a terrific alternative is a cricket.
This adorable chirper—whose six-to-eight-week life
span is a fine match for a four-year-old's attention
span—is certainly easier to raise than a canary,
requires a much smaller cage, and never scatters
seeds on the floor. In fact, if there *are* seeds on the
floor—or anything else, for that matter—this om-
nivorous pet will enjoy them as dinner. One of nature's
more modest diners, a cricket can probably feed on a
single large green bean for life.

SMALL AND SMART

All things being relative, ants are a snap to raise.
There are about six thousand different kinds to
choose from, and you can house an entire colony
between two plastic lids of refrigerator dishes taped
together. Best of all, they're wonderful role models for
kids. Ants are industrious, clean themselves without
being reminded, and have a sense of direction that
could put homing pigeons to shame. And as far as
feeding goes, they need only a few drops of water and
bits of juicy food daily to be happy as clams—which,
incidentally, also make good (if boring) pets.

A REAL PLAYMATE

For an active child who wants a real playmate, there is
always the kangaroo. The small wallaby type is best,

since a large full-size one might not fit through your doorway.

Kangaroos are vegetarians, so you never have to worry about their jumping up and snatching a roast from the table. And being grazers, they can eat their dinner and do your lawn at the same time. Additionally, if your neighbor needs to borrow it for a while, you can train the kangaroo to return itself.

NO WINDING REQUIRED

Kids who enjoy mechanized toys usually take great delight in turtles. And turtles have several advantages: there's no assembly required, and they never need winding or batteries. They can also go from room to room, carrying things on their back. The North American box turtle is a real winner. It can support two hundred times its own weight, which means that a twenty-pounder could easily help you move the piano.

LOW-MAINTENANCE PETS

Hibernating animals can be a boon to working mothers. De-scented skunks (which make adorable pets) will, if quartered outdoors, go underground as soon as the thermometer registers 50° or less for several days in succession (adult males hang on until the real deep freeze sets in) and stay there for six to twelve weeks. That's like not having a pet and having one too! Other hibernators that you might want to consider because they'll leave you free to travel during the winter holiday season are toads, woodchucks, badgers, and raccoons. Of course, if nothing furry, feathered, four-footed, or scaly seems low-maintenance enough, you can always buy your kid a geranium and call it Spot!

It is always impolite to correct a boss's pronunciation—especially of his or her name.

—POWERMOM PROVERB

POWERMOMETIQUETTE

The trouble with books of etiquette is that, basically, they're written for people who don't need them. Women who throw formal dinner parties for diplomats and heads of state *know* how to meet, greet, and eat correctly. They don't need to be told that it's bad form to cool champagne in a thermos or to use the baby's hot plate as a serving dish for peas. Their guidelines are carefully drawn and followed.

Not so, though, for working mothers, whose quandaries of protocol spring from awkward everyday situations that no reputable arbiter of etiquette would want to deal with. But since these situations do exist, working mothers should know how to handle them correctly.

GROCERY SHOPPING WITH YOUR CHILD

Turning your chores into quality time with your child can be very rewarding; it can also be socially devastating. Supermarket etiquette is a tricky business. If your child is small enough to fit into the seat of a shopping cart, it is not only proper but sensible to keep the kid sitting there right through to checkout;

but it is gauche to resort to handcuffs or Krazy-Glue in order to do so.

It is perfectly acceptable for your child to munch on some animal crackers while riding around the market; it is in poor taste to allow her to deposit the uneaten portion of any cookie—or the box—in someone else's basket. It is in worse taste to allow the kid to sneak the half-empty box back onto the shelf.

If your child manages to topple a large pyramid of soup cans or cereal boxes, it is not necessary for you to restack them, but it is courteous to inform the store manager of the accident. It is not impolite to be wearing dark glasses while you make your report.

When you're at the checkout counter with a very large order and a child in tow, and the person behind you has a single container of milk, it is considered rude not to let the person go before you—but only by people who have never had to shop with a kid.

VISITING A CO-WORKER'S NEW BABY

When visiting someone with a new baby, it is expected that you inquire about the child's feeding and sleeping habits, and no matter how unremarkable they are, to say otherwise. Responding to whatever the mother tells you with "Wow! That's incredible!" is always in order.

If the child's mother asks, "Would you like to hold the baby?" and you'd really rather not, the socially permissible response is "I'd love to but I have a terrible cold," though "I'm such a butterfingers" will work equally well. These are strictly honorable white lies, especially if the baby has just been fed and you've come straight from the office and are wearing your best silk blouse.

HANDLING YOUR BABY'S VISITORS

Just because friends come to see your baby, it is not necessary to pass the infant around as if he or she were a tray of hors d'oeuvres. (It is good manners, though, to have something to pass around, such as a tray of hors d'oeuvres.)

If, during the visit, some friend or relative thinks it's cute to pinch the baby's nose, you may politely—and wisely—snatch your child away. This can be done in the traditional manner ("Goodness, it's time for Billy's nap already!") or by slipping a clothespin on the pincher's nose and asking, "How do *you* like it?" Either is correct, though the latter will give you a lot more satisfaction.

CHILDREN'S BIRTHDAY PARTIES

Invitations may be sent, telephoned, or transmitted verbally at school. As far as etiquette is concerned, all are equally correct; as far as *you're* concerned, only the supervised sending of written invitations is advisable. (Nothing short of two heels breaking simultaneously will disorient you faster than thirteen extra little arrivals your kid forgot to tell you he'd invited.)

The birthday cake may or may not be served before the opening of presents, depending on how many children have already tasted the icing with their fingers and how much of a formed cake is left. Candles should be removed immediately after they're blown out to prevent ingestion by small children and show-offy ten-year-olds.

It's perfectly proper to allow a birthday party to run for more than two hours. But it is not recommended.

DEALING WITH YOUR CHILD'S FRIENDS

It is neither correct nor necessary for you to discipline your child's friends, since discipline is a parent's prerogative. But there are exceptions—as when your child's playmates decide to use your bed as a trampoline, or when a kid's idea of "fooling around" suddenly necessitates a fire extinguisher, Band-Aids, ice packs, a sling, stitches, or the S.W.A.T. team.

MEETING YOUR CHILD'S TEACHER

It is eminently proper to introduce yourself since, strong family resemblances aside, you are taller than your child, and incidences of mistaken identity can result in embarrassing confusion about your child's progress. Even if you expect a bad report, it's poor form to pretend to be just a concerned neighbor, or offer the teacher a bribe.

If you differ with the teacher's opinions, it's perfectly correct to say so, providing you do so in language acceptable in school classrooms. It's passé to remark that your child "never does that at home," since teachers hear this all the time—and don't believe it anyway.

Shopping for children's clothes is an experience somewhat akin to going through a car wash without your car. —POWERMOM PROVERB

COPING WITH CLOTHES-SHOPPING FOR KIDS

Buying clothes for children is one of those rite-of-passage ordeals mothers are, unfortunately, subjected to on a regular basis. It is a task that challenges the rules of order by which our universe functions. But you can protect yourself from befuddlement, self-doubt, and innumerable headaches if you recognize one essential fact: children's clothing sizes are the invention of a deranged manufacturer's cartel.

IN THE BEGINNING

Inside each article of infant's clothing is a little tag—not unlike those the law forbids you to remove from sofas, pillows, and reclining chairs—ostensibly designed to guide you in proper fitting. Since babies don't have hip, bust, waist, or shoulder measurements to speak of, manufacturers, in obvious desperation, have sized their goods in terms of a baby's age, weight, and sometimes height. They might just as well have provided guidelines based on eye color.

Let's take the Newborn label, for example. Reason dictates that Newborn is the size you'd want for baby's first months. But reason, you have to keep in mind, has no part in the buying of children's clothes. This becomes evident when you discover that each manufacturer has very definite and different ideas about how long and fat your newborn should be.

If your baby is a hefty ten-pounder, the child will be out of luck when it comes to getting clothes. Too big for the Newborn size, too short for the next, he will be relegated to that floppy-footed, slack-sleeved look one associates with performing animals and cute actresses dressed in men's striped pajamas. Salespeople seem to favor this look; they'll rarely recommend buying clothing that actually fits a child. Most mothers just resign themselves to having their kids dressed six months to two years ahead of their time.

Baby clothes run from Newborn to 24 Months. When the child reaches the age of two years (approximately thirty-six to thirty-eight inches, thirty-three to thirty-six pounds, according to manufacturers' specs), he—ready or not—enters a brand-new sizing bracket called Toddler.

Toddler sizes run from 2T to 4T. Now you might reason that a 24 Months size should be the same as a 2T, but with kids' clothing, reason has to be kept at bay: 2T is bigger than 24 Months. The sizes are not only unidentical, but often can't be found in the same department. And this is only the beginning of the bizarre division of children's clothes. To be forewarned helps (but not much).

KNOW YOUR TIMES TABLES

There is a 4 to 6X category for girls, and a 4 to 7 category for boys. (No one knows why girls have the X and boys don't. Conceivably, it has something to do with chromosomes.) Then comes the 7 to 14 range for girls, and the 8 to 14 grouping for boys. After that, the 3 to 13 Juniors for girls, and the 12 to 20 Students for boys.

Though the numbers seem as though they correspond to the child's age, they have virtually nothing to do with it. A six-year-old girl might wear a size 8, while her twelve-year-old sister wears a size 5. And to make things really confusing, the twelve-year-old can save her size 4 for the six-year-old to grow into! (Even Pythagoras could go nuts trying to figure out those progressions!)

THE TRUTH ABOUT SMALL, MEDIUM, AND LARGE

Getting the hang of number sizing is a breeze compared with dealing with the alternatives, namely Small, Medium, and Large. You can't truly appreciate the lunacy of S's, M's, and L's until you've had to select one of them for your child. It makes you wonder if any of the manufacturers have ever seen a kid off the drawing board. And if any have, they obviously haven't told the others about it. There is apparently an unwritten law that no two manufacturers use the same guide for these categories. What's Small for one is Large for another; Medium can run either way. Actually, Medium is a halfhearted corporate concession to temporarily deranged mothers. One chooses it in desperation.

In coping with S, M, and L, keep in mind that they are your enemies. Think of them in the way you do plaque or germs, things that you must defend against. Your best protection is to keep your child with you at all times when shopping. Then S, M, and L can't fool you with their seductive simplicity. But without a kid on hand, you're easy prey.

IMPORT INSANITY

Once you get into foreign-made clothing, you become a pushover for tranquilizers. I do think someone ought to send a few kids overseas just to be measured! I don't think anyone there has the vaguest idea of what sizing's about. The price may be right, but that's about it. I bought my petite eight-year-old niece an imported sweater labeled M, and she looked as though she'd been body-wrapped in an elastic bandage.

If you need a Large, forget it. You either get a tent—some sort of overcompensation—or a roomy wrap for a Barbie doll.

As for conversion charts, well, something awful must happen at the international dateline, because these charts are no help at all. This is true for goods imported from Korea, Taiwan, Britain, France, Israel, the Philippines, Monaco, Egypt, Sierra Leone, and any other place separated from us by a large body of water. The only logical conclusion is that kids over there in no way resemble ours—or the whole thing is some sort of protest against American foreign policy.

CONSIDERING THE OTHER ALTERNATIVES

Companies that manufacture children's clothing are aware that sizing scales are inadequate. For this reason, and no doubt to prevent rowdy and dangerous protests, they persist in placating us with guidelines: Slim, Regular, and Husky are examples.

Your daughter might look slim to you, but put her in a pair of Slim jeans in her usual size, and she could run the risk of gangrene. (Though there is no proof, it's suspected that the mannequins used for patterns are skeletons from a medical college.) If you need a Slim or Husky and can't find it, just subtract or add two numbers to the size you're looking for and get a Regular. It helps to carry a calculator or a small abacus.

Perhaps the most insidious development in the manufacture of children's clothing has been the creation of stretch fabrics. The Orwellian overtones of "One Size Fits All" are distressing—and the phrase itself is patently untrue. All men might be created equal, but all leotards aren't. Some of these omnifitting tights will come up to your kid's armpits, while others will never make it past the navel. And aside from the fact that the things don't fit, the idea that your child can't wear what's purported to be a universal size can be psychologically damaging.

THE SHOEMAKER'S CHILDREN ALWAYS NEED THEM—BUT SO DO YOURS

Children's feet, unlike those of any other animal, grow at a financially exorbitant rate. (Studies have shown that if a mother of two had left her children unshod for the past fifteen years, she could now own a condominium on Ibiza.)

Shoe sizes, like clothing sizes, are totally absurd. They start conventionally at 1 and go to 13. But just when children begin taking pride in numbers, when they fully believe that bigger numbers mean better things, they find they've gone from 12½ back to 1. It's discouraging for them, and a step closer to breakdown for you. Why can't sizes go on consecutively? What's so bad about wearing a size 29½ shoe?

SOCKING IT TO YOU

The worst thing about footwear is socks. They make no sense at all. Despite the fact that shoes and socks cover the same appendages, their sizes have nothing in common. If your daughter wears a size 3 sneaker, for reasons beyond any normal human's power of speculation she'll need a size 7–9½ sock. And this is one thing you *must* accept on faith. Nobody, but nobody, gets to try on socks. Children can try on gloves all day long, but socks—never. You would think someone would reverse the rules. Most mothers usually know where their kids' feet have been since morning, but they couldn't vouch for their hands.

If it were up to me, all children would be born with fur. It would thicken in winter, thin in summer (you could give the kids baths and do your laundry at the same time), then fall off when they were old enough to shop for their own clothes.

Any child with an inquiring mind will soon find your hidden Polaroids. —POWERMOM PROVERB

HOW TO ANSWER THOSE IMPOSSIBLE QUESTIONS KIDS ASK

For some reason unknown to etymologists, psychologists, and certainly mothers, the moment children learn the deceptively innocuous interrogative "why," they are in possession of a three-letter lethal weapon and verbal power capable of shattering saintly patience, steel nerves, and, occasionally, good dishes (if they happen to be around at the time).

I'm not talking about the "why" in "Why is the sky blue?" or "Why is the snow white?" or even "Why do firemen wear red suspenders?" Those are legitimate queries. They're the reason for encyclopedias and libraries; they give meaning to the suggestion "Look it up."

No, I'm talking about the other "why," the one that augurs migraines, that has the power to propel placid mothers into dizzying altitudes of anxiety, that precedes such questions as "Why can't I drink root beer for breakfast?" or "Why can't I have a dog?" or "Why must I do it?" and inestimable frustrating others. Those are the questions that can never be answered to a child's satisfaction and invariably force you to resort to the irritating response you hated when you were a kid, that infamous parental cop-out: "Just because I say so!"

Take, for instance, the classic "Why do I have to go to bed now?" This one has been around since the beginning of bedtime, and children down through the generations have evolved an awesome capacity for parrying any and all reasonable responses to it.

To _H.M._ Time _4:05_ A.M.☐ P.M.☒
Date _3/15_

WHILE YOU WERE OUT

M _Your Son_

of

Phone

	Area Code		Number	Extension	
TELEPHONED		☒	PLEASE CALL		
CALLED TO SEE YOU			WILL CALL AGAIN		
WANTS TO SEE YOU			URGENT		
		RETURNED YOUR CALL			

Message _Went to Eric's house. Going to try out the hang gliders they made out of Hefty bags._

Operator _LG_

A FAMILIAR SCENARIO

INTERIOR LIVING ROOM. NIGHT.
CHILD is sprawled on couch watching television.
YOU stand tapping your wristwatch.

CHILD: Gee, Mom, it's only nine-thirty. Why do I have to go to bed now?

YOU: Because there's school tomorrow and you need your rest.

CHILD: I stayed up later than this when we went to Aunt Rita's—and *that* was a school night.

YOU *(defensively)*: That was different. That was a special occasion.

CHILD: Tonight Godzilla meets the Bionic Woman. That's a special occasion.

The kid has you there.

YOU *(your voice rising)*: Look, I don't care if Godzilla meets *God* tonight. There's school tomorrow and you're going to bed.

CHILD *(undaunted)*: But why do I have to go to bed now?

YOU: I just told you.

CHILD: But when we went to Aunt Rita's—

YOU *(cutting child off angrily)*: That's enough about Aunt Rita's. You're going to bed this minute.

CHILD: But why do I have—

YOU *(shouting)*: Just because I say so!

You stand there, furious with yourself for once again being reduced to the humiliation of pulling rank.

DISSOLVE TO BLEAK

However, it doesn't have to work out this way. As a Powermom, I've discovered how to respond to unanswerable questions: *with unquestionable answers!*

THE SAME FAMILIAR SCENARIO, WITH AN UNQUESTIONABLE ANSWER

INTERIOR LIVING ROOM. NIGHT.
CHILD *is sprawled on couch watching television.*
YOU *stand smiling.*

> CHILD: Gee, Mom, it's only nine-thirty. Why do I have to go to bed now?

> YOU: Because your mattress closes in five minutes, that's why.

The response is so unexpected and so unequivocally off-the-wall that the child has absolutely no way to counter it. We know that though it may not be effective in getting the kid to sleep, it will preclude further argument.

END

INSTANT IMPOSSIBLE-QUESTION ANSWER GUIDE

Squelching a no-win dialogue with a kid is a learned art. But once you get the hang of it, you can become a verbal Picasso.

Impossible Question	Unquestionable Answer
✽ "Why do I have to get a haircut?"	✽ "Because it's too long to stuff the pillows."
✽ "Why can't I wear jeans to the dance?"	✽ "Because they're blue and cover your legs."

✲ "Why can't Mike stay for dinner?"	✲ "For medical reasons."
✲ "Why won't you let me ride my bike in the rain?"	✲ "Because we can't afford it."
✲ "Why can't I watch TV while I do my homework?"	✲ "Because you can't make soup in a pothole."
✲ "Why can't we go to the movies?"	✲ "Because it's too dark inside."
✲ "Why can't I have a cookie?"	✲ "Because you might put it in your mouth."
✲ "Why do I have to mow the grass?"	✲ "To prevent forest fires."
✲ "Why do I have to eat my spinach?"	✲ "Because it's green and already dead."
✲ "Why do I have to take a bath?"	✲ "Because the tub feels empty without you."

By using unquestionable answers consistently, you'll find that in time your kids will tire of asking impossible questions and begin sticking to more manageable queries like "Why do volcanoes erupt?" or "Why do trees lose their leaves in the fall?" Of course, when reference sources are unavailable and the kids demand an immediate answer, you might have to fall back on "Just because I say so!"

Any toy that's marked "some assembly required"
really means "engineering degree essential."
—**POWERMOM PROVERB**

TOYS THAT CAN HARM YOU

Few activities are potentially more dangerous than choosing toys for children. Sure, hang gliding and eating wild mushrooms have risk factors, but you're aware of those. It's only the rare, enlightened parent who knows the real hidden hazards of children's toys. What you have to understand is that simply because a toy has received a Good Housekeeping Seal of Approval, clearance from *Consumer Reports*, a clean slate from the federal government, Walt Disney, Ralph Nader, and Mr. Rogers doesn't mean it's safe for *you*.

WHAT TO AVOID

Dolls that perform bodily functions

Any doll that can eat, drink, cry, or wet will usually do so . . . on your new rug, new attaché case, new neighbor. . . . As a general rule, if it ballet dances— okay; if it burps—forget it!

Remote control or computerized vehicles

It is thoroughly disconcerting to walk into an empty room and be attacked at the ankles by a truck. It can also be extremely messy if you're carrying a cup of coffee, extremely expensive if you're carrying crystal, and extremely dangerous if you're carrying your kid's baby brother. In short, steer clear of any toy that doesn't require the presence of a kid, or wants to do its own thing.

Toys that take water internally

Little fishies that can be filled up to squirt in the bathtub can, when you're not looking, be filled up and squirted in your briefcase. The same is true of water pistols. Only they can, in the wrong hands, be filled with everything from milk to mouthwash and be fired indiscriminately at targets ranging from the canary to the baby-sitter.

Microscopes

Allegedly "educational," these can set children on biological rampages. Once youngsters get their hands on those sterile pincers and little glass slides, everything in the house is in for scientific scrutiny. They'll pull hair from their heads, from the dog, from their siblings. They'll bring in scrunched spiders, fly wings, beetles, things you wouldn't touch with a ten-foot pole, let alone a two-inch pincer. Don't feel guilty about standing in the way of science. Louis Pasteur did all right, and he never had a microscope when he was a kid.

Binoculars and telescopes

These can come in handy on camping trips or when observing shooting stars, but camping trips and shooting stars are limited—other people's windows are not. If the child is really interested in birds or constellations, you're better off taking the kid to the zoo or the planetarium.

Musical toys

Unless your child is seriously interested in music and/or truly gifted in this area (we're talking Mozart, okay?), it is foolish and very masochistic of you to buy the kid an instrument. It's downright hostile for someone else to.

"Just-Like-Daddy's" tool kits

Equipped with a variety of nonfunctional plastic screwdrivers, hammers, and wrenches, these kits can't fix anything! Aside from teaching your child state-of-the-art incompetence, they can bring a kid to levels of frustration matched only by those of a real daddy when looking for his real tools.

"Just-Like-Mommy's" kitchen appliances

Unlike "Just-Like-Daddy's" tool kits, these are usually functional, which means they not only require adult supervision but adult cleaning as well. If that isn't enough of a deterrent to their purchase, keep in mind that anything your kid bakes, blends, or freezes in an ice tray, you're going to have to eat (or at least pretend to). And if this still doesn't sound too bad to you, you've never experienced Tollhouse cookies made by an eight-year-old who's used olives in place of chocolate chips.

Giant riddle and pun books

Harmless? Ha! Just leave a child alone with one of these for an hour and you're in for a year's worth of groaners. ("What happens to a duck when he flies upside down?" "He'll quack up.") And those Knock-Knocks? You'll take more than Joe Frazier, Muhammad Ali, and Rocky I, II, and III combined!

Video games

No matter which ones, they're all insidious. Aside from their incessant mechanical beeps (which often send you rushing to the kitchen thinking that a timer or the microwave has gone off), they're designed to undermine parental abilities and engender Pavlovian responses in children—causing them to crave quarters when in darkened rooms or within viewing distance of flashing lights.

Birds and bees have as much to do with the facts of life as black nightgowns do with keeping warm.
—POWERMOM PROVERB

TEACHING THE FACTS OF LIFE

It seems that one of the biggest problems in teaching kids the facts of life is that most parents become uneasy when talking to their children about anything that in any way involves the removal of clothing—which, in the case of reproduction, often does. Not with birds and bees, of course, which could account for their popular use as examples in discussions about sex.

But teaching a child the facts of life doesn't have to be an awkward encounter. Facts of life are just *facts*. And if they're handled that way, honestly and straight-forwardly, there's no problem. For example:

✳ It is a fact that when water gets very cold it can freeze.

✳ It is a fact that when butter gets very warm it can melt.

✳ It is a fact that when a man and woman have sex, one of them can become pregnant.

✳ It's as simple as that. And the following Do's and Don'ts Guide should make it even simpler.

POWERMOM FACTS OF LIFE GUIDE

✻ DO tell children the truth. You can't say to a child at age three that the stork brings babies and then sock him at five with sexual intercourse. Talk about losing credibility! The kid won't even take your word on how to make Jell-O after that!

✻ DON'T give personalities to parts of the body. Thinking that anthropomorphizing genitalia or things like sperms and eggs makes the reproductive process more comprehensible to children is a great mistake. My sister described sperm to her son as aggressive little tadpoles, and the kid is still convinced that when he fathers a child, it's going to be Kermit the Frog.

✻ DO wait until your child shows an interest in the subject. Children mature at their own pace, so there's no *right* time to teach them about sex (though sometime before the age of twenty-one is advisable). But dragging a kid away from her favorite TV show because you feel ready to explain how daddy plants his seed will only cause problems. As extraordinary as conception is, nine out of ten seven-year-olds would rather watch the end of "Happy Days."

✻ DON'T discuss the birds and bees. This can cause significant confusion in a youngster's mind, fostering erroneous beliefs about cross-pollination and eliciting embarrassing and inappropriate responses to honey.

✻ DO discuss masturbation. DON'T demonstrate.

✻ DO use proper terms. This gives youngsters the chance to fall back on the dictionary or encyclopedia when they're confused, bored, or want to impress their friends. (Give some leeway to street and school jargon, just so that the child knows what's being discussed.)

✻ DON'T let the discussion be a solemn or emotionally charged affair. This can imbue sex with all the appeal of rabies shots.

✻ DON'T limit the discussion to how babies are born. On the other hand, don't digress so much that the child thinks you're talking about nuclear disarmament.

Note: It is not necessary to get into S & M or bondage if the child still can't tie his shoelaces.

Never take a kid seriously, if you can take her to school instead.   —POWERMOM PROVERB

WHEN YOU SHOULD KEEP YOUR CHILD HOME FROM SCHOOL

Working mothers always seem to be plagued with indecision and doubt when it comes to keeping a child home from school. Obviously, if the youngster is running a fever, covered with spots (which can't be attributed to a Magic Marker), writhing in pain, or unable to eat a cornflake without intestinal repercussions, there's no decision to make, and the child stays home. But often the situations are not as clearly defined, and then—whether the child is kept home or sent to school—the mother spends her day awash with guilt, wondering if she's made the right decision. The following list has been designed to alleviate this predicament.

Definitely keep your child home from school ✳ ✳ ✳

✳ on holidays

✳ after midnight

* if she keeps a bag over head for three days
* if he receives a death threat from his teacher
* if *you* receive a death threat from his teacher
* if school lunch walks off the plate
* if child's pets are required for science experiments
* during an appendicitis attack
* during a nuclear attack
* if carrying a contagious disease
* if carrying an automatic weapon

Seek and you shall find everything—except, maybe, the mate to your kid's sock.

—POWERMOM PROVERB

FORETELLING WHAT YOUR CHILD WILL BE

In every child there is a grown-up Somebody—a doctor, a lawyer, a hairdresser, a chef. From the moment your baby is born, the clues begin to unfold— the trick is to interpret them correctly.

Not that this is necessary, by any means; some parents like surprises. But think of how helpful it would be if you knew the direction in which your child was headed. You could buy the right toys and books and provide truly useful entertainments. After all, why should you waste precious free time making boring trips to science museums and knock yourself out helping with calculus homework if you know right from the start that your kid will become a rug salesman?

This knowledge is not impossible. The clues *are* there. All you have to do is spot and translate them.

To find out what sort of Powermom detective you are, give yourself the following quiz.

1. Your child is a precocious eighteen-month-old who can recognize all the letters of the alphabet. When

you point to the writing on a box of cereal, the child can say each letter aloud.
Your child will most likely be . . .
(**a**) a writer
(**b**) a lexicographer
(**c**) an optometrist

2. Your child is a finicky eater, capable of pushing a single pea around on a plate for an entire mealtime, abhors anything lumpy, green, or incompatible with peanut butter.
Your child will most likely be . . .
(**a**) anorexic
(**b**) a drag at dinner parties
(**c**) a food critic

3. Your child is fascinated with sizes and shapes of human bodies.
Your child will most likely be . . .
(**a**) a doctor
(**b**) another Richard Simmons or Jane Fonda
(**c**) a success on Seventh Avenue in ladies' coats and dresses

4. Your child can convince you more than once that the reason for a poor grade is that the teacher made a mistake and forgot to include the last test, or that no one in the class got a higher mark.
Your child will most likely be . . .
(**a**) a politician
(**b**) a used-car salesperson
(**c**) a lawyer

5. Your child has terrible handwriting, tells corny jokes at the wrong time, and is never around when needed.
Your child will most likely be . . .
(**a**) a parking lot attendant

(**b**) your brother-in-law
(**c**) a doctor

6. Your child is fascinated by animals and spends lots of time petting the family cat.
Your child will most likely be . . .
(**a**) a veterinarian
(**b**) a zoo keeper
(**c**) a furrier

To __H. M.__ Time __4:45__ A.M.☐ P.M.☐
Date __5/1__

WHILE YOU WERE OUT

M __your son__

of _____

Phone _____

Area Code	Number	Extension

			PLEASE CALL	✗
TELEPHONED			WILL CALL AGAIN	
CALLED TO SEE YOU			URGENT	
WANTS TO SEE YOU				
	RETURNED YOUR CALL			

Message __"It wasn't my fault."__

Operator __L. G.__

7. Your child has a Socratic proclivity for riddles.
Your child will most likely be . . .
(**a**) a Zen master
(**b**) a psychotherapist
(**c**) the crossword puzzle editor of *The New York Times*

8. Your child is in the habit of saying lavish good-nights ("Good night, fishy!" "Good night, clock!" Good night, door!").
Your child will most likely be . . .
(**a**) the last guest to leave a party
(**b**) a night watchman
(**c**) a strong contender for anchorperson on the evening news

9. Your child continually interrupts what you're saying to finish the statement in his own words and often asks you a question and then answers it himself.
Your child will most likely be . . .
(**a**) a district attorney
(**b**) a bore
(**c**) a talk show host

10. Your child is prone to exaggeration; tells you that the new girl in class has a dog as big as a house, a house as big as a castle, and more money than Yoko Ono and Paul McCartney combined, when in fact the kid has a Lhasa apso, the house is an A-frame, and her parents own the car wash.
Your child will most likely be . . .
(**a**) a pathological liar
(**b**) an unsuccessful systems analyst
(**c**) a great PR person

11. Your child can tell you quite matter-of-factly that the toilet has just overflowed, ruined the carpet from bathroom to playroom, and short-circuited the TV, and that Billy is "having some minor difficulty" giving mouth-to-mouth resuscitation to the hamster.
Your child will most likely be . . .
(**a**) a presidential press secretary
(**b**) a salesperson at Macy's
(**c**) a pilot

12. Your child enjoys dressing up in costumes and excels at imitations—mimicking friends, celebrities, animals, machines, and musical instruments with equal gusto.
Your child will most likely be . . .
(**a**) a comedian in Las Vegas
(**b**) a transvestite in San Francisco
(**c**) an FBI agent

13. Your child can eat bagels, pizza, grits, souvlaki, mulligan stew, and egg rolls with equal enthusiasm, and rarely wears a coat in January.
Your child will most likely be . . .
(**a**) fat
(**b**) fun to travel with
(**c**) president

To learn how you scored, turn to page 122.

Answers

1. **(c)**. If you chose **(a)** you should realize that the earmarks of a fledgling writer are much clearer—staring out of windows a lot, being prone to good and bad days, having the habit of scribbling one or two things on a piece of paper and then scrunching it up and starting over.

2. **(c)**. **(a)** and **(b)** are possibilities.

3. **(c)**.

4. **(a)**, **(b)**, and **(c)** are all correct.

5. **(c)**. And the child probably prefers golf tournaments to "Sesame Street" too.

6. **(c)**.

7. **(a)**, **(b)**, and **(c)** are equally correct.

8. **(c)**.

9. **(c)**.

10. **(c)** and/or **(a)**.

11. **(c)**, but the kid has a good shot at **(a)**.

12. **(c)**.

13. **(a)**, **(b)**, and **(c)**.

PART 3

THINKING OF YOU! YOU! YOU!

Powermom Hall of Fame

How to Stop Dressing for Failure
Instant Clothing Power ✲ Bringing Home the Bacon
House Dressing ✲ Authority Dressing ✲ Sexcess Dressing
Flunk-proof Fashion Guidelines

A Powermom's Sex Manual
How's Your Sex Life? ✲ Inability to Achieve Privacy
Premature Expectation ✲ Fear of Falling ✲ Dealing with
Importance ✲ Income Compatibility

How to Meet a Man
Get into Recycling ✲ Timing Is Important ✲ Your Best
Approach ✲ How to Spot the Married Ones
Sporting Propositions ✲ Smart Shopping
Using Public Transportation ✲ If You Want to Meet . . .

**Great New Do-It-Yourself Plans for
Renovating Your Man**
Save That Male ✻ Anyone Can Do It ✻ Find the Trouble Spots
Fixing Fading Romance ✻ Serious Repairs
Important Points to Remember

The All-Natural Anxiety Diet
Creative Implementation of Natural Appetite Suppressants
Use Everyday Aggravations as Reducing Aids
How Your Children Can Help You Shape Up ✻ Meal Avoidance
How to Succeed at Anxiety Dieting

Recommended Reading List

Questions That Working Mothers Ask Most Often

POWERMOM HALL OF FAME

Moses's mother
Jesus's mother
Tiberius's mother
Whistler's mother
Portnoy's mother
Bambi's mother
Ma Barker
Ma Kettle
Ma Bell
Mama Leone
Mother Teresa
Mother Nature
Mother Earth
Queen Victoria
Rose Kennedy
Ethel Kennedy

(YOUR NAME HERE)

POWERMOM FASHION TIP:
*Never carry a shopping bag if you can get
someone to carry it for you.*

HOW TO STOP DRESSING FOR FAILURE

As a working mother, you haven't time to learn the intricate couture-contriving that's been devised for dressing for success, but you *can* learn how to stop dressing for failure! What's required is simply the recognition that clothes are both tools and weapons and, like all tools and weapons, are not only useless but potentially harmful if used improperly.

INSTANT CLOTHING POWER

Whether you work for a high-powered, big-city ad agency, a small-town insurance firm, or behind the counter at a Seven-Eleven store, there will come a time when you'll want a promotion, a raise, or both. Sure, it's nice to believe that your ability and good attendance record are what matter—but it's nice to believe in the Tooth Fairy also. The reality is that if you want more money and a better position, you will have to ask for them; and when you do, you're going to need *instant clothing power*.

In business, instant clothing power means a smart

blouse or dress with short sleeves. That's right, *short*. These have psychological impact: a show of arms. Employers know that a woman who can fashionably bare arms is not to be trifled with. (Barbara Walters allegedly wore short sleeves when she negotiated her million-dollar TV contract; and, according to some palace sources, Lady Di was in a sleeveless dress when Prince Charles proposed.) Basic pumps, a simple belt, and a necklace are fine accessories, provided the necklace isn't made out of macaroni by one of your kids.

BRINGING HOME THE BACON

Instant clothing power is not the same in all life areas. For instance, a svelte short-sleeved dress might impress a boss, but it won't get you anywhere with a butcher. A nubby gray sweater worn over another gray sweater and an overly long dark skirt with an uneven hemline is the outfit that gets results there. It's the sort of old-country look that keeps butchers honest— the look of a woman who sniffs a chicken to see if it's fresh, and complains no matter what the price. If you've been going to the market in designer jeans and coming home with steaks that are tough enough to drive through a vampire's heart, it's definitely time to change your image.

HOUSE DRESSING

Clothes, believe it or not, can also mean the difference between beautiful shiny floors and overwaxed dull ones. This has been proved conclusively in hundreds of TV commercials, countless magazine ads, and in my own home.

I used to wear any old clothes around the house. My sons would often rush off to school without breakfast, my fried chicken would occasionally come out greasy, my oven never really got clean, spots never came out of the kids' shirts, and our cat was a finicky eater. I tried new breakfast cereals, new cooking oils, new oven cleaners, new detergents, and new cat foods, but nothing worked. Then one day, morosely leafing through a magazine that showed pictures of smiling mothers eating breakfast with their kids, standing beside glistening ovens, sorting spot-free laundry, I realized what I'd been doing wrong: I had been dressing for failure.

None of the smiling mothers in the magazine was wearing a torn "I Love New York" T-shirt or her husband's old jogging suit. They were in shirtwaist dresses or plaid shirts and pressed jeans. I immediately went out and bought myself a plaid shirt and pressed my jeans, and my family has had hearty breakfasts, crisp chicken, spotless laundry, and a fat cat ever since.

AUTHORITY DRESSING

Jeans and pullovers are fine to wear when playing games with your kids, driving them to friends' homes, or going out for burgers and shakes, but such outfits have absolutely no wardrobe clout when it comes to laying down house rules. If you dress like a teenager, you're going to command about as much respect as one (unless, of course, you dress like the Fonz, which isn't easy considering the price of leather jackets these days). But if you dress like an authority figure, it's a whole different story. To get my kids to shape up, I dress like Darth Vader. Basic black from head to toe.

Works every time. But any outfit that looks like a uniform will be effective, especially with just the right accessories, such as a yardstick or a riding crop.

Note: Even animals respond to authority dressing. If your dog pulls you down the street every time you take him for a walk, try wearing black and tan. This gives you a sort of tough, no-nonsense, Doberman air. You'll be amazed at how your dog will no longer give you so much as a tug.

To _H. M._ Time _3:15_ A.M.☐ P.M.☐
Date _2/29_

WHILE YOU WERE OUT

M _your babysitter_

of _____

Phone _____

Area Code	Number	Extension	☒
TELEPHONED	☒	PLEASE CALL	
CALLED TO SEE YOU		WILL CALL AGAIN	
WANTS TO SEE YOU		URGENT	
	RETURNED YOUR CALL		

Message _Thinks there might be a small leak in waterbed. Wants to know where galoshes are._

Operator _L. G._

SEXCESS DRESSING

How to stop dressing for failure in the bedroom is another matter entirely. The right clothes, whether on or off, can mean the difference between a night of passion and . . . well, just a night. Black nightgowns are the sexiest, but only if you leave the light on—white is your best bet in the dark. Wear pink only if you're under twenty-five, yellow only if it's a gift from your husband or his mother; green is okay for the holiday season, but reserve red for those *special* occasions. Of course, when you have a headache, wear striped pajamas. On the other hand, if it's your husband who has the headache, you might as *well* wear striped pajamas!

FLUNK-PROOF FASHION GUIDELINES

✻ Always have on hand several short-sleeved outfits in assertive colors for dealing with bosses, baby-sitters, bill collectors, and in-laws. (Assertive colors are policemen blue, warden gray, nurse white, and surgeon green.)

✻ Have at least one outfit in a conciliatory shade for making up with husbands, lovers, kids, bosses, baby-sitters, and in-laws. (Conciliatory colors are baby blue, pixie pink, and puppy beige.)

✻ For entertaining, purchase only clothes that look as if they stain easily. (If you wear fabrics that are obviously wash-and-wear, you're going to find yourself in the kitchen all evening.)

✻ Set aside one frayed blouse and skirt for when the kids ask for allowance raises.

* Avoid wearing a seat belt after parking your car.
* Never let good taste, your budget, fashion magazines, loved ones, or common sense dictate your wardrobe.

The best thing you can say about the average working mother's sex life is that it's not time-consuming. —POWERMOM PROVERB

A POWERMOM'S SEX MANUAL

With all the research that's been done by Masters and Johnson, all the volumes of instructive literature available on intimacy—to say nothing of the discovery of the Grafenberg Spot and the invention of the hot tub—you would think that sex problems would be a thing of the past for almost everyone. Well, not so.

Working mothers operate under sexual handicaps that aren't even mentioned, let alone explained, in manuals on the subject. Oh, sure, it's easy to tell a woman that she can enhance her sensuality and spark her love life by preparing a candlelight dinner and greeting her man at the door in something diaphanous or slinky. But if you're a working mother, you're lucky if you have enough energy left at day's end even to *get* to the door. Besides, chances are the kids will still be awake, badgering you with questions about why you're in your nightclothes, blowing out the candles as soon as you light them, and inevitably putting you in a mood that is about as romantic as anticipating an audit by the IRS.

But with a workable formula, sex problems are no more difficult to solve than math problems. (In fact, the latter are much trickier, especially if you're dealing with fractions or trying to balance your checkbook.) To begin, an evaluation of your sex life is in order.

HOW'S YOUR SEX LIFE?

Do you ✲✲✲

	YES	NO
✲ Find that testing your kids on their spelling words is inadequate foreplay?	____	____
✲ Have difficulty becoming aroused when you roll over in bed on your child's Legos?	____	____
on your child's Play-Doh?	____	____
on your child?	____	____
✲ Feel that your job interferes with your sex life?	____	____
between nine and five?	____	____
✲ Become distracted during sex by the sound of your kids watching TV?	____	____
in the same room?	____	____
✲ Find that the sexiest outfit you now own is a low-cut sweat suit?	____	____
a regular sweat suit?	____	____
✲ Have difficulty expressing your sexual desires to your partner?	____	____
over the phone?	____	____
during a business meeting?	____	____
in a note on the kitchen bulletin board?	____	____
✲ Think that Joan Rivers has a better sex life?	____	____
Joan of Arc?	____	____

✳ Feel that if you surprised your partner with a candlelight dinner, the
first thing he'd ask is if you'd forgotten to pay the electric bill?

YES   NO

_____ _____

✳ Think your love life could get a
PG rating?   _____ _____
a G rating?   _____ _____

✳ Remember the last time you had an
orgasm?   _____ _____
faked an orgasm?   _____ _____
thought about an orgasm?   _____ _____

If you answered "yes" to two or more of the above
questions, you are in a sexual slump that requires
immediate attention. Sexual slumps are not uncom-
mon (captive pandas have them quite often), but they
can be unpleasant and very distressing, especially if
you're in one all the time!

INABILITY TO ACHIEVE PRIVACY

Probably the most widespread cause of sexual slump-
ing among working mothers is being unable to achieve
privacy. This detriment to sexual fulfillment often
promotes high-level frustration and usually stems
from the presence of children—though it can be
caused by the presence of in-laws, repair persons, and
large pets.

Every woman is physically capable of achieving
privacy, and any working mother can learn how with a
little daily practice. Simply accustom children (in-
laws, repair people, pets, etc.) to the idea that you
don't have to account for your absence during their
every waking moment. This can be accomplished by
slipping away to the bedroom (or the attic or the

closet) for a few not-to-be interrupted moments, moments that you extend day by day until a private time-period is established. It helps if your partner practices this exercise too, and is even more effective if he practices it with you, as achieving privacy alone is not nearly as rewarding as doing so together.

PREMATURE EXPECTATION

Planning a romantic evening brightens a working mother's day, but assuming things will go as planned can be dangerous. Premature expectation is a common sexual pitfall, especially among young working mothers who have not yet learned that the greater their desire for a perfect love night, the more likely their child is to come down with the flu. Obviously this can take its toll on the libido and promote feelings of resignation—as well as a hunger for the carefree past and anything chocolate.

To prevent premature expectation and its consequences, it's best to restrict your consumption of romantic novels (I've yet to read one where the heroine's tide of passion was stemmed by her kid's inflamed tonsils), and it's preferable to avoid making reservations at a love nest that requires an unrefundable deposit.

FEAR OF FALLING

Surprisingly, a large sexual stumbling block for the *single* working mother is not fear of flying but fear of falling—falling in love with someone who is incompatible with her children, her job, her schnauzer; or, concomitantly, falling *out* of love with someone who *is* compatible with her children, her job, and her schnauzer.

This is not an irrational fear, but it is counterproductive to a rich and rewarding sex life. If you're a single working mother, your fear of falling can be eradicated by an awareness of basic romantic no-no's. Avoid intimate entanglements with your boss, your boss's husband, the father of your child's best friend, the father of your child's worst enemy, and anything with an expiration date or that requires batteries.

DEALING WITH IMPORTANCE

Don't let your career ruin your love life. Just because you're an executive and used to bringing work home doesn't mean that you have to bring it to bed with you. (You bring milk home and don't bring that to bed with you.) Studies have shown that foreplay is considerably foreshortened by intimate contact with profit and loss statements, inter-office memos, bar graphs, and dictaphones.

INCOME COMPATIBILITY

This problem increases daily as more and more women find better jobs and their income rises. But the fact that yours is bigger than his is no cause for locked libidos. Money should be kept out of the bedroom unless you're a professional.

The process of meeting men is no more difficult than meeting trains or loan payments or any of life's other challenges—only it's a lot more fun to meet a man than a loan payment.

—Powermom proverb

HOW TO MEET A MAN

To be successful at anything, you should think positively, which means—in the case of connecting with the opposite sex—abandoning the belief that every man you meet will most likely be either married or gay. In the first place, it is not so; in the second, that's just the sort of negative thinking that can keep a single working mother alone with a Kleenex box on more weekends than she'd care to contemplate.

GET INTO RECYCLING

Unlike Siberian tigers and ten-cent candy bars, men are not an endangered species. There are plenty to go around. Think of all the women you know who have recently gotten divorced. Their ex's haven't disappeared. From my former office alone, during the past year seven males have been put back into circulation. Multiply this by thousands of other offices across the country, and you'll have an idea of how many available guys there really are.

Just because a man wasn't right for one woman doesn't mean he won't be right for you. Everyone's taste is different. Right now, somewhere in New Jersey, a nice lady is living happily with my ex-husband. She calls him "huggy bear" and "cuddles," which are nothing like the names I called him, but it does show you the advantages of recycling. In fact, if you think of men in the same way you think of discount coupons, you realize that what your neighbor might have absolutely no use for could be just what you need, and vice versa. In other words, the quiet introverted bore you've been dating might be someone else's strong silent dream man. By canvassing friends to find out if they're really happy with the men in their lives, you can set up some remarkably satisfying co-operative exchanges. (See also "Great New Do-It-Yourself Plans for Renovating Your Man.")

TIMING IS IMPORTANT

One of the easiest ways to meet men is by never wearing a watch. This simple omission on your wrist provides boundless opportunities to approach males without seeming forward, loose, or desperate. What could be more proper than asking for the time? As soon as it's been established, be it 8:04 or 6:45, the object is to prolong the moment. Doing something unexpected, such as opening your purse and producing a baby bunny or a revolver, usually accomplishes this.

Once the conversation is in motion, you can take it as far as your imagination and scruples allow. Admittedly, this involves a bit of chicanery, but deception is used in nature all the time. During mating season, some insects go so far as to change their shapes!

YOUR BEST APPROACH

The best way to approach a man is from the front. This not only gives you a chance to get a better look at him, but gives him the opportunity to take a good look at you. It also prevents the possibility of being mistaken for a mugger or pickpocket and getting punched in the stomach.

An exception to using the frontal approach is when you're at museums or art galleries. In these institutions, sidling is more advantageous, especially if the man is looking at a work of art. By aligning yourself with him shoulder to shoulder, you'll feel confidently equal and can unobtrusively initiate conversation. A hushed "Pretend you don't know me" or a sincere "Isn't it wonderful what a high-protein diet can accomplish?" will under most circumstances elicit a response.

HOW TO SPOT THE MARRIED ONES

Before you take any conversation too far with a male, it's wise to find out if he's married. Subtlety is important, since men tend to react as favorably to questions about their marital status as they do to Mace. Queries such as "Nice tie . . . did your wife pick it out?" and "Who does the cooking at your house?" should get you the answers you are looking for. If not, you can try any—or all—of the following:

✳ "Live alone?"

✳ "Do you think married men make better lovers?"

✳ "Why is it that every single guy I meet is married?"

✳ "Have you ever discussed bodily functions with your in-laws?"

SPORTING PROPOSITIONS

Obviously, the more men gathered in a given place, the better your chances are for meeting one. But because there are fewer and fewer situations these days where males outnumber females, and unless you can look casual hanging out in a men's locker room or intend to join the army, your widest selection will probably be at a sporting event. Showing up at the Y on the wrong night also offers good possibilities.

SMART SHOPPING

For unmarried working mothers whose only free time is a lunch hour, shoe stores can be as romantically rewarding as singles bars. Shoe salespersons are predominantly male, generally well mannered, and at your feet for as long as you want them to be. If at first you don't succeed in arousing the salesman's interest, you can always try on another pair of shoes.

Sporting goods stores can have pretty nifty-looking sales help too. One woman I know found that by simply asking about casting reels, she could hold a salesman's interest long enough to fish for his marital status and drop in a line about her own.

Other good bets: computer shops; electronics outlets; and auto, plumbing, and electrical supply stores.

USING PUBLIC TRANSPORTATION

Probably nothing can be more conducive to instant intimacy than sharing a seat on a public conveyance. Needless to say, the longer the ride, the more mileage you can get out of the seating arrangement. The hitch is selecting the right seat partner. Swiftness is essential, along with a keen and discerning eye. She who hesitates usually winds up looking addled or drunk— and, quite often, standing. To tone up, practice strategic seat moves whenever and wherever you can—in movie theaters, on park benches, trains, planes, sampans, gondolas. Before long you should be able to size up the prospects on a crowded crosstown bus in ten seconds flat, and will have more men on call than the National Guard.

To _H. M._ Time _11:20_ A.M.☐ P.M.☐
Date _10/31_

WHILE YOU WERE OUT

M _Mrs. Stanislaus'_
of _your gynecologists'_
Phone _office_

Area Code	Number	Extension

TELEPHONED	☒	PLEASE CALL	
CALLED TO SEE YOU		WILL CALL AGAIN	☒
WANTS TO SEE YOU	☒	URGENT	
		RETURNED YOUR CALL	

Message _The rabbit died._

Operator _L. G._

✲ A BANK PRESIDENT

An easy get-acquainted method is to overdraw your account, protest that it's the bank's error, and keep protesting until you're introduced to the man at the top. You still have to pay the extra charges, but if the bank president is single, and you're lucky, it will certainly be worth it.

✲ A STOCKBROKER

This can be a risky proposition because it usually requires a small investment, which might or might not pay off in more ways than one.

✲ A DOCTOR

Just go to a theater and faint.

✲ A LAWYER

Try to get called for jury duty, or sue someone.

✲ A POLICEMAN

There are several ways to go about this. You can park in a No Stopping zone and stay in your car, go through a red light, buy a radar detector and exceed the speed limit when you hear the beep, or, if you're desperate, commit a small crime (felonies are not recommended).

✲ A PSYCHIATRIST

Either use the conventional method of having a nervous breakdown, or try something more creative:

crash a VFW convention and flashdance in a bikini with a rubber chicken strapped to your thigh.

✳ AN ACCOUNTANT

List outrageous deductions on your income tax return. You'll find yourself in a room full of accountants before you know it.

✳ AN ACTOR

Go to any restaurant in New York or Los Angeles and strike up a conversation with the best-looking, least-adept waiter.

No man is an island—or a piece of cake either.
                                    —POWERMOM PROVERB

GREAT NEW DO-IT-YOURSELF PLANS FOR RENOVATING YOUR MAN

If you're bored with the man in your life, have had it up to here with coming home to a partner who gazes deep into your eyes only when he's asking you why he doesn't have any clean socks, or long for someone who can look at a sunset through the living-room window without remarking that it needs washing, it's time you did something about it. Stop daydreaming about separation (it can be traumatic) or divorce (it can be expensive) or finding another guy (it can be trouble), and start making your dreams come true by renovating the man you have!

SAVE THAT MALE

There is absolutely no reason for any working mother to cast off a perfectly good male just because of a few flaws. Look at it this way: if you had an old oak bureau with some unattractive marks on it, you wouldn't just chuck it, would you? Of course not. If you did, you'd find that someone else would grab it, refinish it, and wind up with a showpiece that you could kick yourself for ever letting out of your home. The same holds true for discarding a worn male. Before you could say, "I'm glad he's out of my life," another woman would have him in hers, set right to work on refurbishing him, and end up with the Mr. Right *you* always wanted.

ANYONE CAN DO IT

Even working women, with limited free time, are doing wonderful things with secondhand males these days. (If you think Nancy Reagan's most challenging renovation project was the White House, you're mistaken.) The point is, don't let someone take advantage of the groundwork you've already put in. Why let a total stranger claim benefits that are rightfully yours? With a little guidance, patience, and perhaps some new after-shave, you can remodel your man in your own home—and before it's too late. In most cases, such remodeling is no more difficult than re-covering a sofa or—depending on the man— rewiring a home computer.

FIND THE TROUBLE SPOTS

To begin, search out the specific areas in which your particular man is in need of repair or refinishing. Then tackle those areas one by one. (Considering them all together tends to overwhelm beginners; this is a common pitfall—it prevents many domestic renovation projects from ever getting off the ground.)

FIXING FADING ROMANCE

Romance is usually the first thing to wear thin. No matter how dashing or charming a man might have been originally, overexposure—to marriage, your job, children, bills, football, video games—takes its toll. If now the only reason your man would ever put you up on a pedestal would be so you could clean the top of the kitchen cabinets, and the last time he hugged you was to teach you the Heimlich maneuver, then allow extra hours for work in this area.

If, for example, his idea of an intimate evening for two is a game of gin rummy, strip the house of all playing cards. (Or simply remove two or three cards from each deck. Your kids can help you do this, sometimes without your even asking.) The next step is to surprise him by suggesting something so outrageously intimate that he'll never take you for granted again. For instance, something like flossing each other's teeth.

Firelight and candles are always appropriate, even if they do make it difficult to locate those hard-to-reach areas.

SERIOUS REPAIRS

Serious men have been quite the rage in life and literature for centuries. But if your current man makes Hamlet look like Milton Berle, and considers pleasure a waste of time, then some solid overhauling is called for. And it's not as time-consuming as you might think.

One of the most common and annoying problems women have with serious men is that they moan about things. But like squeaks in doors, moans from men can be eliminated with do-it-yourself know-how.

Let's just say that your man moans while reading the morning or evening newspaper. This can darken the mood of any room he's in (which is particularly irksome if you've just had your whole place repainted or spent an entire Saturday washing windows to let in more light). But your problem is not insoluble. Before he sees the paper, fold it to double thickness and fill it with melon rinds, empty tomato-paste cans, cucumber peels, and any other garbage you have around. Then bring up the sides of the paper, twist, secure with a rubber band or metal tie-strip, and deposit the package in your trash can. As an alternative, you can use the entire paper to line the cat's litter box. If you haven't a cat, roll the newspaper up and toss it in front of your neighbor's door.

Sometimes moans occur because the cap has been left off the toothpaste. This is easily rectified by the purchase of tooth powder or baking soda, both of which can be found at your local supermarket.

IMPORTANT POINTS TO REMEMBER

* Don't worry about small annoying habits. All men have them; that's the way they're made.

* Before getting involved in any domestic renovation, take into account that some men, like some furniture, are beyond amateur reclamation, and if this is the case, you're better off getting rid of your man and starting from scratch.

* There are a lot of used males out there, so you don't have to take the first one you find.

You know you have a weight problem when someone says, "Six carats"—and all you can think of is lunch. —POWERMOM PROVERB

THE ALL-NATURAL ANXIETY DIET

Have you been on enough crash diets to consider yourself a nutritional safety hazard? Tried to lose weight by drinking more water in a day than bedouins see in a month? Made meals entirely of celery? Eaten enough hard-boiled eggs to acquire a lasting hostility toward chicken? Gone from "Scarsdale" to "Beverly Hills" and back and still can't close the zipper on your jeans? It's time, then, to try the Powermom's All-Natural Anxiety Diet. In fact, by just *being* a Powermom, you'll start shedding pounds instantly.

Note: Unlike other quick weight-loss regimens, the Anxiety Diet requires no calorie counting, no carbohydrate deprivation, no willpower, and—best of all—no additional book purchase.

CREATIVE IMPLEMENTATION OF NATURAL APPETITE SUPPRESSANTS

This is the primary element of Anxiety Dieting. No matter how compulsive an eater you are, there are always some moments when you're not hungry—during surgery, in the middle of an important job interview, while skydiving, scuba diving, etc. Unfortunately, such antihunger usually fades by the next mealtime. But not if you know how to recapture it. Recapturing antihunger is no more difficult than remembering your zip code. The easiest way is to use the same sense-memory technique employed by method actors. Take a few minutes before each meal and think back to those occasions when eating was the last thing on your mind:

* the eight-hour, unair-conditioned car trip with grandma, the kids, and the dog, when the temperature hit a record high . . .

* the evening of the Fourth of July picnic when you discovered that the mayo in the potato salad had gone bad . . .

* the day you lost your best friend's diamond earrings . . .

* the night you found the tank's missing goldfish . . .

* the morning after New Year's Eve . . .

* your son't first overnight hike . . .

* your last request for a raise . . .

The more vividly you recreate the memory, the more diminished your appetite. (I've found that I now can pass up any dessert by simply taking time out for a little Proustian recall of a flight I took to Chicago when "slight turbulence" turned out to be Hurricane David.)

USE EVERYDAY AGGRAVATIONS AS REDUCING AIDS

You'll be astonished at how unappealing your favorite meals become if, before dinner, you—

* read the newspaper or watch the news and pay special attention to stories on pesticides, carcinogens, mass murders, and toxic waste

* total up all the money you regret having spent during the year*

* pay bills**

* look and see what the cat brought in

* clean out the refrigerator

* read the sealed note your child brought home from her teacher

* get an estimate on what it will cost to repair the car

* get on the scale

* discover a half-drunk cup of coffee that's gone unnoticed for more than a week

* retrieve anything that was once edible from under your kid's bed

* call your ex-husband

* see your ex-husband

*This causes an intense churning in your stomach that can burn up approximately one to four calories per dollar, so even if you do manage to clean your plate, the actual caloric count will be only half. In effect, you can treat yourself to a three-ounce T-bone steak that will be no more fattening than a large scoop of cottage cheese.

**This also causes calorie-cutting stomach churning; but if you're low on funds, it can actually perk up your spirits, because the greater the discrepancy between your bank balance and your minimum payments, the more weight you will lose.

HOW YOUR CHILDREN CAN
HELP YOU SHAPE UP

With Anxiety Dieting, kids are natural reducing aids—just allow them to make dinner. You'll find it's easy to pass up pasta when it's been prepared by an eight-year-old who thinks *al dente* means "still crunchy." Mashed potatoes your weakness? You'll find they leave you completely cold once you see your kids mashing them with their hands.

(*Hint:* If you've staunchly proclaimed that under no circumstances is the refrigerator to serve as a morgue for biology-class specimens, you might want to rescind your dictum. Few sights can discourage snacking faster than a glimpse of a freeze-dried frog next to the cheesecake.)

For exercise, toddlers are about the best waist trimmers around. Stand beside your little one, about three feet away from a low table upon which there is a shiny, breakable object. The moment the child heads for the table, you stretch . . . bend over . . . and pull the kid back. (Children at this age are tireless—and determined—so you'll be able to repeat the exercise at least five times on each side.)

(*Hint:* If the child becomes frustrated and begins bouncing angrily up and down, bounce up and down with him. This is great for the circulation.)

Deep knee bends can become virtually effortless by putting your youngster into a high chair, carriage, or playpen and giving the child something to hold. The kid will continue to drop it as long as you keep picking it up. (For older children, buy a board game that has a lot of little pieces. What will be left on the floor daily should be good for at least twenty deep knee bends.)

MEAL AVOIDANCE

Not eating is, without a doubt, the surest way to lose weight; and foregoing one or two meals a day is particularly easy for working mothers.

* To skip breakfast, sleep half an hour later in the morning, so that you have just enough time to get the kids off to school and nothing more. (*Hint:* To avoid grabbing a doughnut on the way out, store all baked goods behind the Christmas ornaments in the back of the hall closet.)

* To bypass lunch, arrange to have root canal work done for that hour, or brown-bag something that will have no appeal at noon. (It's been shown that working mothers can lose up to five pounds in one work week by sticking to tripe-on-toast sandwiches.) In a pinch, you can always ask a co-worker to lock you in the Xerox room.

* Getting through dinner without eating is tricky, but it can be done by tying your hands behind you.

HOW TO SUCCEED AT ANXIETY DIETING

Like a Japanese tea ceremony or the selection of perfectly ripe tomatoes at the supermarket, truly successful Anxiety Dieting is both a skill and an art. You must—

* train yourself to arrange food uninterestingly on your plate;

* learn to recognize and avoid fine restaurants;

* become adept at hiding leftovers in the back of the

refrigerator where you won't notice them until they're inedible;

✱ break the connection between a dinner table and food by eating at other places, such as the sink, a windowsill, or the dashboard of your car.

How long can you stay on the Anxiety Diet? *As long as you like!* Just keep these guidelines in mind:

1. You can have as many cocktails as you wish—but only for breakfast.

2. Cakes and cookies are allowed—if they're two weeks old.

3. You can eat all the butter and mayonnaise you want—but you can't put it on anything.

4. No salt—except on desserts.

RECOMMENDED READING LIST

Mommie Dearest, by Christina Crawford. (William Morrow, $9.95.) A Hollywood Powermom's daughter reminisces about why her brother was strapped to his bed, why her name was left off her mother's will, and wire hangers.

Rosemary's Baby, by Ira Levin. (Random House, $10.95.) A suspenseful tale of a Powermom's pregnancy, and a wonderfully supportive case for amniocentesis.

Little Gloria: Happy at Last, by Barbara Goldsmith. (Knopf, $15.95.) A clash of Powermoms that results in stretch jeans.

Madame Bovary, by Gustave Flaubert. Translated by Mildred Marmur. (Signet Classics, $2.75.) A potential Powermom in northern France searches for her G spot in vain.

Oedipus the King, by Sophocles. Translated by Stephen Berg and Diskin Clay. (Oxford University Press, $12.95.) A Powermom finds herself in the middle of a whacky case of mistaken identity.

Alice Adams, by Booth Tarkington. (Twentieth Century Press.) When life becomes unglued, a small-town

Powermom pushes for her daughter—a little too hard—and finds that nothing seems to stick.

Mama's Bank Account, by Kathryn Forbes. (Harcourt Brace Jovanovich, $2.95.) An immigrant Powermom's daughter hangs out the family's laundry, sells it to the movies (*I Remember Mama*), and makes a bundle of big bucks.

The World According to Garp, by John Irving. (Dutton, $10.95.) Tongue-in-cheek recollections of life with an outspoken Powermom.

Portnoy's Complaint, by Philip Roth. (Random House, $14.50.) "M" is for the million things she gave him.

QUESTIONS THAT WORKING MOTHERS ASK MOST OFTEN

Q. "Why am I doing this?"

Q. "I wonder if I'll make it through to the weekend?"

Q. "Will drugs make my life easier?"

Q. "Where the hell is the baby-sitter?"

Q. "What's quality time?"

Q. "Does anyone have an aspirin?"

Q. "Why does this always happen when I'm late?"

Q. "Do you think I'm made of money?"

Q. "Why are there feathers in the blender?"

Q. "What did I do to deserve this?"

Q. "Do you want a spanking?"

Q. "Whose idea was it to wash the cat?"

Q. "Are you sure you're talking about *my* child?"

Q. "You want to know why I haven't quit smoking?"

Q. "Do you think I'm doing this for fun?"

Q. "What memo?"

Q. "Haven't you ever heard of soap?"

Q. "Is it my turn in the car pool again?"

Q. "Why do I feel so guilty?"

Q. "Why am I always so tired?"

Q. "Do you mind if we don't tonight?"

EPILOGUE: YOU ARE NOT ALONE

You are not the only working mother who has ever ✳ ✳ ✳

✳ worn a belt made out of aluminum flip-tops to a business meeting.

✳ pretended to enjoy a breakfast of peanut butter and Fruit Loops in bed on Mother's Day.

✳ had to sit through a three-hour movie being explained to you by an eight-year-old.

✳ had to Scotchguard the dog.

✳ hidden in the bathroom to sneak a cigarette.

✳ had to serve your kids' cookies to company.

✳ had to serve your company dinner on your kid's arts-and-crafts project.

✳ broken a promise.

✳ misinterpreted your three-year-old's artwork.

✳ sent a borderline flu case to school.

✳ lied to your child about the reasons for your divorce.

* thrown out a jar of muddy water without knowing it was your kid's science experiment.

* had to watch your child play submarine, do a wheelie, launch a paper airplane from the stairs, and then be accused of missing the important part.

* put your job on the line to play midwife to a gerbil.

* raided a piggy bank.

* missed your child's Christmas pageant.

* cried on the *last* day of school.